C-620　　CAREER EXAMINATION SERIES

This is your
PASSBOOK for...

Process Server

Test Preparation Study Guide
Questions & Answers

COPYRIGHT NOTICE

This book is SOLELY intended for, is sold ONLY to, and its use is RESTRICTED to individual, bona fide applicants or candidates who qualify by virtue of having seriously filed applications for appropriate license, certificate, professional and/or promotional advancement, higher school matriculation, scholarship, or other legitimate requirements of education and/or governmental authorities.

This book is NOT intended for use, class instruction, tutoring, training, duplication, copying, reprinting, excerption, or adaptation, etc., by:

1) Other publishers
2) Proprietors and/or Instructors of "Coaching" and/or Preparatory Courses
3) Personnel and/or Training Divisions of commercial, industrial, and governmental organizations
4) Schools, colleges, or universities and/or their departments and staffs, including teachers and other personnel
5) Testing Agencies or Bureaus
6) Study groups which seek by the purchase of a single volume to copy and/or duplicate and/or adapt this material for use by the group as a whole without having purchased individual volumes for each of the members of the group
7) Et al.

Such persons would be in violation of appropriate Federal and State statutes.

PROVISION OF LICENSING AGREEMENTS – Recognized educational, commercial, industrial, and governmental institutions and organizations, and others legitimately engaged in educational pursuits, including training, testing, and measurement activities, may address request for a licensing agreement to the copyright owners, who will determine whether, and under what conditions, including fees and charges, the materials in this book may be used them. In other words, a licensing facility exists for the legitimate use of the material in this book on other than an individual basis. However, it is asseverated and affirmed here that the material in this book CANNOT be used without the receipt of the express permission of such a licensing agreement from the Publishers. Inquiries re licensing should be addressed to the company, attention rights and permissions department.

All rights reserved, including the right of reproduction in whole or in part, in any form or by any means, electronic or mechanical, including photocopying, recording, or by any information storage and retrieval system, without permission in writing from the Publisher.

Copyright © 2024 by
National Learning Corporation

212 Michael Drive, Syosset, NY 11791
(516) 921-8888 • www.passbooks.com
E-mail: info@passbooks.com

PUBLISHED IN THE UNITED STATES OF AMERICA

PASSBOOK® SERIES

THE *PASSBOOK® SERIES* has been created to prepare applicants and candidates for the ultimate academic battlefield – the examination room.

At some time in our lives, each and every one of us may be required to take an examination – for validation, matriculation, admission, qualification, registration, certification, or licensure.

Based on the assumption that every applicant or candidate has met the basic formal educational standards, has taken the required number of courses, and read the necessary texts, the *PASSBOOK® SERIES* furnishes the one special preparation which may assure passing with confidence, instead of failing with insecurity. Examination questions – together with answers – are furnished as the basic vehicle for study so that the mysteries of the examination and its compounding difficulties may be eliminated or diminished by a sure method.

This book is meant to help you pass your examination provided that you qualify and are serious in your objective.

The entire field is reviewed through the huge store of content information which is succinctly presented through a provocative and challenging approach – the question-and-answer method.

A climate of success is established by furnishing the correct answers at the end of each test.

You soon learn to recognize types of questions, forms of questions, and patterns of questioning. You may even begin to anticipate expected outcomes.

You perceive that many questions are repeated or adapted so that you can gain acute insights, which may enable you to score many sure points.

You learn how to confront new questions, or types of questions, and to attack them confidently and work out the correct answers.

You note objectives and emphases, and recognize pitfalls and dangers, so that you may make positive educational adjustments.

Moreover, you are kept fully informed in relation to new concepts, methods, practices, and directions in the field.

You discover that you are actually taking the examination all the time: you are preparing for the examination by "taking" an examination, not by reading extraneous and/or supererogatory textbooks.

In short, this PASSBOOK®, used directedly, should be an important factor in helping you to pass your test.

PROCESS SERVER

DUTIES AND RESPONSIBILITIES
Assists in serving all process and legal documents for the District Attorney's Office to appropriate persons; serves papers in a variety of actions at law; assists in supervising a group of subordinate process servers; assists with security functions; performs related duties as required.

EXAMPLES OF TYPICAL TASKS
Makes personal service of legal process and supervises a group of subordinate process servers in the personal service of summonses, subpoenas, mandatory orders, or other legal papers; effects service of ordinary legal papers on attorneys for parties involved in litigation, its agents and officers; may serve notices of appeal, orders with notice of entry, orders to show cause, and papers of similar nature, upon attorneys for litigants; may file papers including records on appeal and briefs in the local courts; makes investigations to locate people on whom process is to be served and, when necessary, makes affidavits or appears in court to testify as to the service of process; assigns or records the assignment of process serving workloads to subordinate process servers; keeps appropriate records of completed work; performs related work as required.

SCOPE OF THE EXAMINATION
The written test will cover knowledge, skills and/or abilities in such areas as:

1. Applying written information (laws, rules, regulations, procedures, etc.) in civil law enforcement;
2. Evaluating information and evidence;
3. Understanding and interpreting written material;
4. Preparing written material; and
5. Office record keeping.

HOW TO TAKE A TEST

I. YOU MUST PASS AN EXAMINATION

A. WHAT EVERY CANDIDATE SHOULD KNOW

Examination applicants often ask us for help in preparing for the written test. What can I study in advance? What kinds of questions will be asked? How will the test be given? How will the papers be graded?

As an applicant for a civil service examination, you may be wondering about some of these things. Our purpose here is to suggest effective methods of advance study and to describe civil service examinations.

Your chances for success on this examination can be increased if you know how to prepare. Those "pre-examination jitters" can be reduced if you know what to expect. You can even experience an adventure in good citizenship if you know why civil service exams are given.

B. WHY ARE CIVIL SERVICE EXAMINATIONS GIVEN?

Civil service examinations are important to you in two ways. As a citizen, you want public jobs filled by employees who know how to do their work. As a job seeker, you want a fair chance to compete for that job on an equal footing with other candidates. The best-known means of accomplishing this two-fold goal is the competitive examination.

Exams are widely publicized throughout the nation. They may be administered for jobs in federal, state, city, municipal, town or village governments or agencies.

Any citizen may apply, with some limitations, such as the age or residence of applicants. Your experience and education may be reviewed to see whether you meet the requirements for the particular examination. When these requirements exist, they are reasonable and applied consistently to all applicants. Thus, a competitive examination may cause you some uneasiness now, but it is your privilege and safeguard.

C. HOW ARE CIVIL SERVICE EXAMS DEVELOPED?

Examinations are carefully written by trained technicians who are specialists in the field known as "psychological measurement," in consultation with recognized authorities in the field of work that the test will cover. These experts recommend the subject matter areas or skills to be tested; only those knowledges or skills important to your success on the job are included. The most reliable books and source materials available are used as references. Together, the experts and technicians judge the difficulty level of the questions.

Test technicians know how to phrase questions so that the problem is clearly stated. Their ethics do not permit "trick" or "catch" questions. Questions may have been tried out on sample groups, or subjected to statistical analysis, to determine their usefulness.

Written tests are often used in combination with performance tests, ratings of training and experience, and oral interviews. All of these measures combine to form the best-known means of finding the right person for the right job.

II. HOW TO PASS THE WRITTEN TEST

A. NATURE OF THE EXAMINATION

To prepare intelligently for civil service examinations, you should know how they differ from school examinations you have taken. In school you were assigned certain definite pages to read or subjects to cover. The examination questions were quite detailed and usually emphasized memory. Civil service exams, on the other hand, try to discover your present ability to perform the duties of a position, plus your potentiality to learn these duties. In other words, a civil service exam attempts to predict how successful you will be. Questions cover such a broad area that they cannot be as minute and detailed as school exam questions.

In the public service similar kinds of work, or positions, are grouped together in one "class." This process is known as *position-classification*. All the positions in a class are paid according to the salary range for that class. One class title covers all of these positions, and they are all tested by the same examination.

B. FOUR BASIC STEPS

1) Study the announcement

How, then, can you know what subjects to study? Our best answer is: "Learn as much as possible about the class of positions for which you've applied." The exam will test the knowledge, skills and abilities needed to do the work.

Your most valuable source of information about the position you want is the official exam announcement. This announcement lists the training and experience qualifications. Check these standards and apply only if you come reasonably close to meeting them.

The brief description of the position in the examination announcement offers some clues to the subjects which will be tested. Think about the job itself. Review the duties in your mind. Can you perform them, or are there some in which you are rusty? Fill in the blank spots in your preparation.

Many jurisdictions preview the written test in the exam announcement by including a section called "Knowledge and Abilities Required," "Scope of the Examination," or some similar heading. Here you will find out specifically what fields will be tested.

2) Review your own background

Once you learn in general what the position is all about, and what you need to know to do the work, ask yourself which subjects you already know fairly well and which need improvement. You may wonder whether to concentrate on improving your strong areas or on building some background in your fields of weakness. When the announcement has specified "some knowledge" or "considerable knowledge," or has used adjectives like "beginning principles of..." or "advanced ... methods," you can get a clue as to the number and difficulty of questions to be asked in any given field. More questions, and hence broader coverage, would be included for those subjects which are more important in the work. Now weigh your strengths and weaknesses against the job requirements and prepare accordingly.

3) Determine the level of the position

Another way to tell how intensively you should prepare is to understand the level of the job for which you are applying. Is it the entering level? In other words, is this the position in which beginners in a field of work are hired? Or is it an intermediate or advanced level? Sometimes this is indicated by such words as "Junior" or "Senior" in the class title. Other jurisdictions use Roman numerals to designate the level – Clerk I, Clerk II, for example. The word "Supervisor" sometimes appears in the title. If the level is not indicated by the title, check the description of duties. Will you be working under very close supervision, or will you have responsibility for independent decisions in this work?

4) Choose appropriate study materials

Now that you know the subjects to be examined and the relative amount of each subject to be covered, you can choose suitable study materials. For beginning level jobs, or even advanced ones, if you have a pronounced weakness in some aspect of your training, read a modern, standard textbook in that field. Be sure it is up to date and has general coverage. Such books are normally available at your library, and the librarian will be glad to help you locate one. For entry-level positions, questions of appropriate difficulty are chosen – neither highly advanced questions, nor those too simple. Such questions require careful thought but not advanced training.

If the position for which you are applying is technical or advanced, you will read more advanced, specialized material. If you are already familiar with the basic principles of your field, elementary textbooks would waste your time. Concentrate on advanced textbooks and technical periodicals. Think through the concepts and review difficult problems in your field.

These are all general sources. You can get more ideas on your own initiative, following these leads. For example, training manuals and publications of the government agency which employs workers in your field can be useful, particularly for technical and professional positions. A letter or visit to the government department involved may result in more specific study suggestions, and certainly will provide you with a more definite idea of the exact nature of the position you are seeking.

III. KINDS OF TESTS

Tests are used for purposes other than measuring knowledge and ability to perform specified duties. For some positions, it is equally important to test ability to make adjustments to new situations or to profit from training. In others, basic mental abilities not dependent on information are essential. Questions which test these things may not appear as pertinent to the duties of the position as those which test for knowledge and information. Yet they are often highly important parts of a fair examination. For very general questions, it is almost impossible to help you direct your study efforts. What we can do is to point out some of the more common of these general abilities needed in public service positions and describe some typical questions.

1) General information

Broad, general information has been found useful for predicting job success in some kinds of work. This is tested in a variety of ways, from vocabulary lists to questions about current events. Basic background in some field of work, such as sociology or economics, may be sampled in a group of questions. Often these are principles which have become familiar to most persons through exposure rather than through formal training. It is difficult to advise you how to study for these questions; being alert to the world around you is our best suggestion.

2) Verbal ability

An example of an ability needed in many positions is verbal or language ability. Verbal ability is, in brief, the ability to use and understand words. Vocabulary and grammar tests are typical measures of this ability. Reading comprehension or paragraph interpretation questions are common in many kinds of civil service tests. You are given a paragraph of written material and asked to find its central meaning.

3) **Numerical ability**
Number skills can be tested by the familiar arithmetic problem, by checking paired lists of numbers to see which are alike and which are different, or by interpreting charts and graphs. In the latter test, a graph may be printed in the test booklet which you are asked to use as the basis for answering questions.

4) **Observation**
A popular test for law-enforcement positions is the observation test. A picture is shown to you for several minutes, then taken away. Questions about the picture test your ability to observe both details and larger elements.

5) **Following directions**
In many positions in the public service, the employee must be able to carry out written instructions dependably and accurately. You may be given a chart with several columns, each column listing a variety of information. The questions require you to carry out directions involving the information given in the chart.

6) **Skills and aptitudes**
Performance tests effectively measure some manual skills and aptitudes. When the skill is one in which you are trained, such as typing or shorthand, you can practice. These tests are often very much like those given in business school or high school courses. For many of the other skills and aptitudes, however, no short-time preparation can be made. Skills and abilities natural to you or that you have developed throughout your lifetime are being tested.

Many of the general questions just described provide all the data needed to answer the questions and ask you to use your reasoning ability to find the answers. Your best preparation for these tests, as well as for tests of facts and ideas, is to be at your physical and mental best. You, no doubt, have your own methods of getting into an exam-taking mood and keeping "in shape." The next section lists some ideas on this subject.

IV. KINDS OF QUESTIONS

Only rarely is the "essay" question, which you answer in narrative form, used in civil service tests. Civil service tests are usually of the short-answer type. Full instructions for answering these questions will be given to you at the examination. But in case this is your first experience with short-answer questions and separate answer sheets, here is what you need to know:

1) Multiple-choice Questions
Most popular of the short-answer questions is the "multiple choice" or "best answer" question. It can be used, for example, to test for factual knowledge, ability to solve problems or judgment in meeting situations found at work.
A multiple-choice question is normally one of three types—
- It can begin with an incomplete statement followed by several possible endings. You are to find the one ending which *best* completes the statement, although some of the others may not be entirely wrong.
- It can also be a complete statement in the form of a question which is answered by choosing one of the statements listed.

- It can be in the form of a problem – again you select the best answer.

Here is an example of a multiple-choice question with a discussion which should give you some clues as to the method for choosing the right answer:

When an employee has a complaint about his assignment, the action which will *best* help him overcome his difficulty is to
- A. discuss his difficulty with his coworkers
- B. take the problem to the head of the organization
- C. take the problem to the person who gave him the assignment
- D. say nothing to anyone about his complaint

In answering this question, you should study each of the choices to find which is best. Consider choice "A" – Certainly an employee may discuss his complaint with fellow employees, but no change or improvement can result, and the complaint remains unresolved. Choice "B" is a poor choice since the head of the organization probably does not know what assignment you have been given, and taking your problem to him is known as "going over the head" of the supervisor. The supervisor, or person who made the assignment, is the person who can clarify it or correct any injustice. Choice "C" is, therefore, correct. To say nothing, as in choice "D," is unwise. Supervisors have and interest in knowing the problems employees are facing, and the employee is seeking a solution to his problem.

2) True/False Questions

The "true/false" or "right/wrong" form of question is sometimes used. Here a complete statement is given. Your job is to decide whether the statement is right or wrong.

SAMPLE: A roaming cell-phone call to a nearby city costs less than a non-roaming call to a distant city.

This statement is wrong, or false, since roaming calls are more expensive.

This is not a complete list of all possible question forms, although most of the others are variations of these common types. You will always get complete directions for answering questions. Be sure you understand *how* to mark your answers – ask questions until you do.

V. RECORDING YOUR ANSWERS

Computer terminals are used more and more today for many different kinds of exams.

For an examination with very few applicants, you may be told to record your answers in the test booklet itself. Separate answer sheets are much more common. If this separate answer sheet is to be scored by machine – and this is often the case – it is highly important that you mark your answers correctly in order to get credit.

An electronic scoring machine is often used in civil service offices because of the speed with which papers can be scored. Machine-scored answer sheets must be marked with a pencil, which will be given to you. This pencil has a high graphite content which responds to the electronic scoring machine. As a matter of fact, stray dots may register as answers, so do not let your pencil rest on the answer sheet while you are pondering the correct answer. Also, if your pencil lead breaks or is otherwise defective, ask for another.

Since the answer sheet will be dropped in a slot in the scoring machine, be careful not to bend the corners or get the paper crumpled.

The answer sheet normally has five vertical columns of numbers, with 30 numbers to a column. These numbers correspond to the question numbers in your test booklet. After each number, going across the page are four or five pairs of dotted lines. These short dotted lines have small letters or numbers above them. The first two pairs may also have a "T" or "F" above the letters. This indicates that the first two pairs only are to be used if the questions are of the true-false type. If the questions are multiple choice, disregard the "T" and "F" and pay attention only to the small letters or numbers.

Answer your questions in the manner of the sample that follows:

32. The largest city in the United States is
 A. Washington, D.C.
 B. New York City
 C. Chicago
 D. Detroit
 E. San Francisco

1) Choose the answer you think is best. (New York City is the largest, so "B" is correct.)
2) Find the row of dotted lines numbered the same as the question you are answering. (Find row number 32)
3) Find the pair of dotted lines corresponding to the answer. (Find the pair of lines under the mark "B.")
4) Make a solid black mark between the dotted lines.

VI. BEFORE THE TEST

Common sense will help you find procedures to follow to get ready for an examination. Too many of us, however, overlook these sensible measures. Indeed, nervousness and fatigue have been found to be the most serious reasons why applicants fail to do their best on civil service tests. Here is a list of reminders:

- Begin your preparation early – Don't wait until the last minute to go scurrying around for books and materials or to find out what the position is all about.
- Prepare continuously – An hour a night for a week is better than an all-night cram session. This has been definitely established. What is more, a night a week for a month will return better dividends than crowding your study into a shorter period of time.
- Locate the place of the exam – You have been sent a notice telling you when and where to report for the examination. If the location is in a different town or otherwise unfamiliar to you, it would be well to inquire the best route and learn something about the building.
- Relax the night before the test – Allow your mind to rest. Do not study at all that night. Plan some mild recreation or diversion; then go to bed early and get a good night's sleep.
- Get up early enough to make a leisurely trip to the place for the test – This way unforeseen events, traffic snarls, unfamiliar buildings, etc. will not upset you.
- Dress comfortably – A written test is not a fashion show. You will be known by number and not by name, so wear something comfortable.

- Leave excess paraphernalia at home – Shopping bags and odd bundles will get in your way. You need bring only the items mentioned in the official notice you received; usually everything you need is provided. Do not bring reference books to the exam. They will only confuse those last minutes and be taken away from you when in the test room.
- Arrive somewhat ahead of time – If because of transportation schedules you must get there very early, bring a newspaper or magazine to take your mind off yourself while waiting.
- Locate the examination room – When you have found the proper room, you will be directed to the seat or part of the room where you will sit. Sometimes you are given a sheet of instructions to read while you are waiting. Do not fill out any forms until you are told to do so; just read them and be prepared.
- Relax and prepare to listen to the instructions
- If you have any physical problem that may keep you from doing your best, be sure to tell the test administrator. If you are sick or in poor health, you really cannot do your best on the exam. You can come back and take the test some other time.

VII. AT THE TEST

The day of the test is here and you have the test booklet in your hand. The temptation to get going is very strong. Caution! There is more to success than knowing the right answers. You must know how to identify your papers and understand variations in the type of short-answer question used in this particular examination. Follow these suggestions for maximum results from your efforts:

1) Cooperate with the monitor

The test administrator has a duty to create a situation in which you can be as much at ease as possible. He will give instructions, tell you when to begin, check to see that you are marking your answer sheet correctly, and so on. He is not there to guard you, although he will see that your competitors do not take unfair advantage. He wants to help you do your best.

2) Listen to all instructions

Don't jump the gun! Wait until you understand all directions. In most civil service tests you get more time than you need to answer the questions. So don't be in a hurry. Read each word of instructions until you clearly understand the meaning. Study the examples, listen to all announcements and follow directions. Ask questions if you do not understand what to do.

3) Identify your papers

Civil service exams are usually identified by number only. You will be assigned a number; you must not put your name on your test papers. Be sure to copy your number correctly. Since more than one exam may be given, copy your exact examination title.

4) Plan your time

Unless you are told that a test is a "speed" or "rate of work" test, speed itself is usually not important. Time enough to answer all the questions will be provided, but this does not mean that you have all day. An overall time limit has been set. Divide the total time (in minutes) by the number of questions to determine the approximate time you have for each question.

5) Do not linger over difficult questions

If you come across a difficult question, mark it with a paper clip (useful to have along) and come back to it when you have been through the booklet. One caution if you do this – be sure to skip a number on your answer sheet as well. Check often to be sure that you have not lost your place and that you are marking in the row numbered the same as the question you are answering.

6) Read the questions

Be sure you know what the question asks! Many capable people are unsuccessful because they failed to *read* the questions correctly.

7) Answer all questions

Unless you have been instructed that a penalty will be deducted for incorrect answers, it is better to guess than to omit a question.

8) Speed tests

It is often better NOT to guess on speed tests. It has been found that on timed tests people are tempted to spend the last few seconds before time is called in marking answers at random – without even reading them – in the hope of picking up a few extra points. To discourage this practice, the instructions may warn you that your score will be "corrected" for guessing. That is, a penalty will be applied. The incorrect answers will be deducted from the correct ones, or some other penalty formula will be used.

9) Review your answers

If you finish before time is called, go back to the questions you guessed or omitted to give them further thought. Review other answers if you have time.

10) Return your test materials

If you are ready to leave before others have finished or time is called, take ALL your materials to the monitor and leave quietly. Never take any test material with you. The monitor can discover whose papers are not complete, and taking a test booklet may be grounds for disqualification.

VIII. EXAMINATION TECHNIQUES

1) Read the general instructions carefully. These are usually printed on the first page of the exam booklet. As a rule, these instructions refer to the timing of the examination; the fact that you should not start work until the signal and must stop work at a signal, etc. If there are any *special* instructions, such as a choice of questions to be answered, make sure that you note this instruction carefully.

2) When you are ready to start work on the examination, that is as soon as the signal has been given, read the instructions to each question booklet, underline any key words or phrases, such as *least, best, outline, describe* and the like. In this way you will tend to answer as requested rather than discover on reviewing your paper that you *listed without describing*, that you selected the *worst* choice rather than the *best* choice, etc.

3) If the examination is of the objective or multiple-choice type – that is, each question will also give a series of possible answers: A, B, C or D, and you are called upon to select the best answer and write the letter next to that answer on your answer paper – it is advisable to start answering each question in turn. There may be anywhere from 50 to 100 such questions in the three or four hours allotted and you can see how much time would be taken if you read through all the questions before beginning to answer any. Furthermore, if you come across a question or group of questions which you know would be difficult to answer, it would undoubtedly affect your handling of all the other questions.

4) If the examination is of the essay type and contains but a few questions, it is a moot point as to whether you should read all the questions before starting to answer any one. Of course, if you are given a choice – say five out of seven and the like – then it is essential to read all the questions so you can eliminate the two that are most difficult. If, however, you are asked to answer all the questions, there may be danger in trying to answer the easiest one first because you may find that you will spend too much time on it. The best technique is to answer the first question, then proceed to the second, etc.

5) Time your answers. Before the exam begins, write down the time it started, then add the time allowed for the examination and write down the time it must be completed, then divide the time available somewhat as follows:
   - If 3-1/2 hours are allowed, that would be 210 minutes. If you have 80 objective-type questions, that would be an average of 2-1/2 minutes per question. Allow yourself no more than 2 minutes per question, or a total of 160 minutes, which will permit about 50 minutes to review.
   - If for the time allotment of 210 minutes there are 7 essay questions to answer, that would average about 30 minutes a question. Give yourself only 25 minutes per question so that you have about 35 minutes to review.

6) The most important instruction is to *read each question* and make sure you know what is wanted. The second most important instruction is to *time yourself properly* so that you answer every question. The third most important instruction is to *answer every question*. Guess if you have to but include something for each question. Remember that you will receive no credit for a blank and will probably receive some credit if you write something in answer to an essay question. If you guess a letter – say "B" for a multiple-choice question – you may have guessed right. If you leave a blank as an answer to a multiple-choice question, the examiners may respect your feelings but it will not add a point to your score. Some exams may penalize you for wrong answers, so in such cases *only*, you may not want to guess unless you have some basis for your answer.

7) Suggestions
   a. Objective-type questions
      1. Examine the question booklet for proper sequence of pages and questions
      2. Read all instructions carefully
      3. Skip any question which seems too difficult; return to it after all other questions have been answered
      4. Apportion your time properly; do not spend too much time on any single question or group of questions

5. Note and underline key words – *all, most, fewest, least, best, worst, same, opposite,* etc.
6. Pay particular attention to negatives
7. Note unusual option, e.g., unduly long, short, complex, different or similar in content to the body of the question
8. Observe the use of "hedging" words – *probably, may, most likely,* etc.
9. Make sure that your answer is put next to the same number as the question
10. Do not second-guess unless you have good reason to believe the second answer is definitely more correct
11. Cross out original answer if you decide another answer is more accurate; do not erase until you are ready to hand your paper in
12. Answer all questions; guess unless instructed otherwise
13. Leave time for review

b. Essay questions
1. Read each question carefully
2. Determine exactly what is wanted. Underline key words or phrases.
3. Decide on outline or paragraph answer
4. Include many different points and elements unless asked to develop any one or two points or elements
5. Show impartiality by giving pros and cons unless directed to select one side only
6. Make and write down any assumptions you find necessary to answer the questions
7. Watch your English, grammar, punctuation and choice of words
8. Time your answers; don't crowd material

8) Answering the essay question

Most essay questions can be answered by framing the specific response around several key words or ideas. Here are a few such key words or ideas:

M's: manpower, materials, methods, money, management
P's: purpose, program, policy, plan, procedure, practice, problems, pitfalls, personnel, public relations

  a. Six basic steps in handling problems:
    1. Preliminary plan and background development
    2. Collect information, data and facts
    3. Analyze and interpret information, data and facts
    4. Analyze and develop solutions as well as make recommendations
    5. Prepare report and sell recommendations
    6. Install recommendations and follow up effectiveness

  b. Pitfalls to avoid
    1. *Taking things for granted* – A statement of the situation does not necessarily imply that each of the elements is necessarily true; for example, a complaint may be invalid and biased so that all that can be taken for granted is that a complaint has been registered

2. *Considering only one side of a situation* – Wherever possible, indicate several alternatives and then point out the reasons you selected the best one
3. *Failing to indicate follow up* – Whenever your answer indicates action on your part, make certain that you will take proper follow-up action to see how successful your recommendations, procedures or actions turn out to be
4. *Taking too long in answering any single question* – Remember to time your answers properly

IX. AFTER THE TEST

Scoring procedures differ in detail among civil service jurisdictions although the general principles are the same. Whether the papers are hand-scored or graded by machine we have described, they are nearly always graded by number. That is, the person who marks the paper knows only the number – never the name – of the applicant. Not until all the papers have been graded will they be matched with names. If other tests, such as training and experience or oral interview ratings have been given, scores will be combined. Different parts of the examination usually have different weights. For example, the written test might count 60 percent of the final grade, and a rating of training and experience 40 percent. In many jurisdictions, veterans will have a certain number of points added to their grades.

After the final grade has been determined, the names are placed in grade order and an eligible list is established. There are various methods for resolving ties between those who get the same final grade – probably the most common is to place first the name of the person whose application was received first. Job offers are made from the eligible list in the order the names appear on it. You will be notified of your grade and your rank as soon as all these computations have been made. This will be done as rapidly as possible.

People who are found to meet the requirements in the announcement are called "eligibles." Their names are put on a list of eligible candidates. An eligible's chances of getting a job depend on how high he stands on this list and how fast agencies are filling jobs from the list.

When a job is to be filled from a list of eligibles, the agency asks for the names of people on the list of eligibles for that job. When the civil service commission receives this request, it sends to the agency the names of the three people highest on this list. Or, if the job to be filled has specialized requirements, the office sends the agency the names of the top three persons who meet these requirements from the general list.

The appointing officer makes a choice from among the three people whose names were sent to him. If the selected person accepts the appointment, the names of the others are put back on the list to be considered for future openings.

That is the rule in hiring from all kinds of eligible lists, whether they are for typist, carpenter, chemist, or something else. For every vacancy, the appointing officer has his choice of any one of the top three eligibles on the list. This explains why the person whose name is on top of the list sometimes does not get an appointment when some of the persons lower on the list do. If the appointing officer chooses the second or third eligible, the No. 1 eligible does not get a job at once, but stays on the list until he is appointed or the list is terminated.

X. HOW TO PASS THE INTERVIEW TEST

The examination for which you applied requires an oral interview test. You have already taken the written test and you are now being called for the interview test – the final part of the formal examination.

You may think that it is not possible to prepare for an interview test and that there are no procedures to follow during an interview. Our purpose is to point out some things you can do in advance that will help you and some good rules to follow and pitfalls to avoid while you are being interviewed.

What is an interview supposed to test?

The written examination is designed to test the technical knowledge and competence of the candidate; the oral is designed to evaluate intangible qualities, not readily measured otherwise, and to establish a list showing the relative fitness of each candidate – as measured against his competitors – for the position sought. Scoring is not on the basis of "right" and "wrong," but on a sliding scale of values ranging from "not passable" to "outstanding." As a matter of fact, it is possible to achieve a relatively low score without a single "incorrect" answer because of evident weakness in the qualities being measured.

Occasionally, an examination may consist entirely of an oral test – either an individual or a group oral. In such cases, information is sought concerning the technical knowledges and abilities of the candidate, since there has been no written examination for this purpose. More commonly, however, an oral test is used to supplement a written examination.

Who conducts interviews?

The composition of oral boards varies among different jurisdictions. In nearly all, a representative of the personnel department serves as chairman. One of the members of the board may be a representative of the department in which the candidate would work. In some cases, "outside experts" are used, and, frequently, a businessman or some other representative of the general public is asked to serve. Labor and management or other special groups may be represented. The aim is to secure the services of experts in the appropriate field.

However the board is composed, it is a good idea (and not at all improper or unethical) to ascertain in advance of the interview who the members are and what groups they represent. When you are introduced to them, you will have some idea of their backgrounds and interests, and at least you will not stutter and stammer over their names.

What should be done before the interview?

While knowledge about the board members is useful and takes some of the surprise element out of the interview, there is other preparation which is more substantive. It *is* possible to prepare for an oral interview – in several ways:

1) Keep a copy of your application and review it carefully before the interview

This may be the only document before the oral board, and the starting point of the interview. Know what education and experience you have listed there, and the sequence and dates of all of it. Sometimes the board will ask you to review the highlights of your experience for them; you should not have to hem and haw doing it.

2) Study the class specification and the examination announcement

Usually, the oral board has one or both of these to guide them. The qualities, characteristics or knowledges required by the position sought are stated in these documents. They offer valuable clues as to the nature of the oral interview. For example, if the job involves supervisory responsibilities, the announcement will usually indicate that knowledge of modern supervisory methods and the qualifications of the candidate as a supervisor will be tested. If so, you can expect such questions, frequently in the form of a hypothetical situation which you are expected to solve. NEVER go into an oral without knowledge of the duties and responsibilities of the job you seek.

3) Think through each qualification required

Try to visualize the kind of questions you would ask if you were a board member. How well could you answer them? Try especially to appraise your own knowledge and background in each area, *measured against the job sought*, and identify any areas in which you are weak. Be critical and realistic – do not flatter yourself.

4) Do some general reading in areas in which you feel you may be weak

For example, if the job involves supervision and your past experience has NOT, some general reading in supervisory methods and practices, particularly in the field of human relations, might be useful. Do NOT study agency procedures or detailed manuals. The oral board will be testing your understanding and capacity, not your memory.

5) Get a good night's sleep and watch your general health and mental attitude

You will want a clear head at the interview. Take care of a cold or any other minor ailment, and of course, no hangovers.

What should be done on the day of the interview?

Now comes the day of the interview itself. Give yourself plenty of time to get there. Plan to arrive somewhat ahead of the scheduled time, particularly if your appointment is in the fore part of the day. If a previous candidate fails to appear, the board might be ready for you a bit early. By early afternoon an oral board is almost invariably behind schedule if there are many candidates, and you may have to wait. Take along a book or magazine to read, or your application to review, but leave any extraneous material in the waiting room when you go in for your interview. In any event, relax and compose yourself.

The matter of dress is important. The board is forming impressions about you – from your experience, your manners, your attitude, and your appearance. Give your personal appearance careful attention. Dress your best, but not your flashiest. Choose conservative, appropriate clothing, and be sure it is immaculate. This is a business interview, and your appearance should indicate that you regard it as such. Besides, being well groomed and properly dressed will help boost your confidence.

Sooner or later, someone will call your name and escort you into the interview room. *This is it*. From here on you are on your own. It is too late for any more preparation. But remember, you asked for this opportunity to prove your fitness, and you are here because your request was granted.

What happens when you go in?

The usual sequence of events will be as follows: The clerk (who is often the board stenographer) will introduce you to the chairman of the oral board, who will introduce you to the other members of the board. Acknowledge the introductions before you sit down. Do not be surprised if you find a microphone facing you or a stenotypist sitting by. Oral interviews are usually recorded in the event of an appeal or other review.

Usually the chairman of the board will open the interview by reviewing the highlights of your education and work experience from your application – primarily for the benefit of the other members of the board, as well as to get the material into the record. Do not interrupt or comment unless there is an error or significant misinterpretation; if that is the case, do not hesitate. But do not quibble about insignificant matters. Also, he will usually ask you some question about your education, experience or your present job – partly to get you to start talking and to establish the interviewing "rapport." He may start the actual questioning, or turn it over to one of the other members. Frequently, each member undertakes the questioning on a particular area, one in which he is perhaps most competent, so you can expect each member to participate in the examination. Because time is limited, you may also expect some rather abrupt switches in the direction the questioning takes, so do not be upset by it. Normally, a board member will not pursue a single line of questioning unless he discovers a particular strength or weakness.

After each member has participated, the chairman will usually ask whether any member has any further questions, then will ask you if you have anything you wish to add. Unless you are expecting this question, it may floor you. Worse, it may start you off on an extended, extemporaneous speech. The board is not usually seeking more information. The question is principally to offer you a last opportunity to present further qualifications or to indicate that you have nothing to add. So, if you feel that a significant qualification or characteristic has been overlooked, it is proper to point it out in a sentence or so. Do not compliment the board on the thoroughness of their examination – they have been sketchy, and you know it. If you wish, merely say, "No thank you, I have nothing further to add." This is a point where you can "talk yourself out" of a good impression or fail to present an important bit of information. Remember, *you close the interview yourself.*

The chairman will then say, "That is all, Mr. _____, thank you." Do not be startled; the interview is over, and quicker than you think. Thank him, gather your belongings and take your leave. Save your sigh of relief for the other side of the door.

How to put your best foot forward

Throughout this entire process, you may feel that the board individually and collectively is trying to pierce your defenses, seek out your hidden weaknesses and embarrass and confuse you. Actually, this is not true. They are obliged to make an appraisal of your qualifications for the job you are seeking, and they want to see you in your best light. Remember, they must interview all candidates and a non-cooperative candidate may become a failure in spite of their best efforts to bring out his qualifications. Here are 15 suggestions that will help you:

1) Be natural – Keep your attitude confident, not cocky

If you are not confident that you can do the job, do not expect the board to be. Do not apologize for your weaknesses, try to bring out your strong points. The board is interested in a positive, not negative, presentation. Cockiness will antagonize any board member and make him wonder if you are covering up a weakness by a false show of strength.

2) Get comfortable, but don't lounge or sprawl

Sit erectly but not stiffly. A careless posture may lead the board to conclude that you are careless in other things, or at least that you are not impressed by the importance of the occasion. Either conclusion is natural, even if incorrect. Do not fuss with your clothing, a pencil or an ashtray. Your hands may occasionally be useful to emphasize a point; do not let them become a point of distraction.

3) Do not wisecrack or make small talk

This is a serious situation, and your attitude should show that you consider it as such. Further, the time of the board is limited – they do not want to waste it, and neither should you.

4) Do not exaggerate your experience or abilities

In the first place, from information in the application or other interviews and sources, the board may know more about you than you think. Secondly, you probably will not get away with it. An experienced board is rather adept at spotting such a situation, so do not take the chance.

5) If you know a board member, do not make a point of it, yet do not hide it

Certainly you are not fooling him, and probably not the other members of the board. Do not try to take advantage of your acquaintanceship – it will probably do you little good.

6) Do not dominate the interview

Let the board do that. They will give you the clues – do not assume that you have to do all the talking. Realize that the board has a number of questions to ask you, and do not try to take up all the interview time by showing off your extensive knowledge of the answer to the first one.

7) Be attentive

You only have 20 minutes or so, and you should keep your attention at its sharpest throughout. When a member is addressing a problem or question to you, give him your undivided attention. Address your reply principally to him, but do not exclude the other board members.

8) Do not interrupt

A board member may be stating a problem for you to analyze. He will ask you a question when the time comes. Let him state the problem, and wait for the question.

9) Make sure you understand the question

Do not try to answer until you are sure what the question is. If it is not clear, restate it in your own words or ask the board member to clarify it for you. However, do not haggle about minor elements.

10) Reply promptly but not hastily

A common entry on oral board rating sheets is "candidate responded readily," or "candidate hesitated in replies." Respond as promptly and quickly as you can, but do not jump to a hasty, ill-considered answer.

11) Do not be peremptory in your answers

A brief answer is proper – but do not fire your answer back. That is a losing game from your point of view. The board member can probably ask questions much faster than you can answer them.

12) Do not try to create the answer you think the board member wants

He is interested in what kind of mind you have and how it works – not in playing games. Furthermore, he can usually spot this practice and will actually grade you down on it.

13) Do not switch sides in your reply merely to agree with a board member

Frequently, a member will take a contrary position merely to draw you out and to see if you are willing and able to defend your point of view. Do not start a debate, yet do not surrender a good position. If a position is worth taking, it is worth defending.

14) Do not be afraid to admit an error in judgment if you are shown to be wrong

The board knows that you are forced to reply without any opportunity for careful consideration. Your answer may be demonstrably wrong. If so, admit it and get on with the interview.

15) Do not dwell at length on your present job

The opening question may relate to your present assignment. Answer the question but do not go into an extended discussion. You are being examined for a *new* job, not your present one. As a matter of fact, try to phrase ALL your answers in terms of the job for which you are being examined.

Basis of Rating

Probably you will forget most of these "do's" and "don'ts" when you walk into the oral interview room. Even remembering them all will not ensure you a passing grade. Perhaps you did not have the qualifications in the first place. But remembering them will help you to put your best foot forward, without treading on the toes of the board members.

Rumor and popular opinion to the contrary notwithstanding, an oral board wants you to make the best appearance possible. They know you are under pressure – but they also want to see how you respond to it as a guide to what your reaction would be under the pressures of the job you seek. They will be influenced by the degree of poise you display, the personal traits you show and the manner in which you respond.

ABOUT THIS BOOK

This book contains tests divided into Examination Sections. Go through each test, answering every question in the margin. We have also attached a sample answer sheet at the back of the book that can be removed and used. At the end of each test look at the answer key and check your answers. On the ones you got wrong, look at the right answer choice and learn. Do not fill in the answers first. Do not memorize the questions and answers, but understand the answer and principles involved. On your test, the questions will likely be different from the samples. Questions are changed and new ones added. If you understand these past questions you should have success with any changes that arise. Tests may consist of several types of questions. We have additional books on each subject should more study be advisable or necessary for you. Finally, the more you study, the better prepared you will be. This book is intended to be the last thing you study before you walk into the examination room. Prior study of relevant texts is also recommended. NLC publishes some of these in our Fundamental Series. Knowledge and good sense are important factors in passing your exam. Good luck also helps. So now study this Passbook, absorb the material contained within and take that knowledge into the examination. Then do your best to pass that exam.

EXAMINATION SECTION

EXAMINATION SECTION
TEST 1

DIRECTIONS: Each question or incomplete statement is followed by several suggested answers or completions. Select the one that BEST answers the question or completes the statement. *PRINT THE LETTER OF THE CORRECT ANSWER IN THE SPACE AT THE RIGHT.*

1. An action is commenced and jurisdiction acquired by service of a(n)

   A. notice of petition
   B. order to show cause
   C. summons
   D. subpoena
   E. notice of appearance

2. Prominently displayed at the top of a summons in an action arising out of a consumer credit transaction is (are) the

   A. words: "class action"
   B. county of residence of the defendent
   C. purchaser, borrower or debtor's credit number
   D. county where the consumer credit transaction took place
   E. words: "consumer credit transaction"

3. A supplemental summons specifying the pleading which must be answered is to be served upon a new party joined in the action when the

   A. joinder is not made upon the new party's motion
   B. joinder is upon the new party's motion
   C. joinder arises out of the action
   D. joinder arises out of a complaint
   E. plaintiff directs the joinder

4. The summons contains, or has attached thereto, a notice stating the object of the action and the relief sought when

   A. a new party is joined in the action
   B. the court deems it as just
   C. the sum of money for which judgment will be taken is uncertain
   D. the complaint is not served with the summons
   E. at all times

5. The court may allow a summons or proof of service of a summons to be amended

   A. before the opening of the action
   B. before the notice of appearance is served
   C. when the answer is served
   D. after the answer and before a reply to a counterclaim
   E. at any time

6. The court may allow any summons or proof of service of a summons to be amended

   A. if the issuing party is not prejudiced of a substantial right
   B. if a substantial right of a party against whom the summons is issued is not prejudiced

2 (#1)

C. upon motion of any party
D. upon notice to the party upon whom the summons was served
E. if the relief sought is not for a sum certain

7. What shall proof of service specify in the event there is no address? 7.____

   A. Last known address
   B. Designated venue
   C. Town, village, or city of service
   D. Place and manner of service
   E. Address unknown

8. It is NOT necessary for proof of service to specify the 8.____

   A. papers served   B. complaint
   C. date of service   D. time of service
   E. address of service

9. Which of the following is *least likely* to be included in the description of the person to whom summons was delivered? 9.____

   A. Age   B. Height and weight
   C. Hair color   D. Attire
   E. Color of skin

10. What is the form of proof of service when service is made by a sheriff? 10.____

    A. Certificate   B. Affidavit   C. Authentication
    D. Deposition   E. Acknowledgment

11. By what method is proof of service made when it is completed by any other person not a sheriff or authorized public officer? 11.____

    A. Certificate   B. Authentication   C. Affidavit
    D. Depostion   E. Acknowledgment

12. A writing admitting service is adequate proof of service when made 12.____

    A. by the person to be served
    B. by the person serving it
    C. and filed with the clerk of the court
    D. by a third party
    E. all of the above

13. Personal service upon the state shall be made by delivering the summons to the 13.____

    A. assistant district attorney or district attorney
    B. secretary of state in the state capital
    C. assistant attorney general at an office of the attorney general
    D. assistant district attorney at an office of the district attorney
    E. secretary of state or his clerk in the offices of the secretary of state

14. Personal service upon the state shall be made by delivering the summons to the proper official in the preceding question 14.____

    A. at any office of the official
    B. at the residence of the official

C. within the county where the state capital is situate
D. within the state
E. within or without the state

15. Proof of personal service upon a natural person shall be filed within _____ day(s) thereafter. 15.____

    A. 1   B. 2   C. 10   D. 20   E. 30

16. Proof of personal service upon a natural person shall be filed with 16.____

    A. any authorized public official
    B. the county clerk of designated venue
    C. the plaintiff or attorney for the plaintiff
    D. the sheriff designated in the summons
    E. the clerk of the court designated in the summons

17. How many day(s) after proof of personal service upon a natural person is service considered complete? 17.____

    A. 1   B. 10   C. 20   D. 30   E. 45

18. Which of the following are methods in which personal service upon a natural person shall be made? Delivering the summons 18.____
    I. within the state to the person to be served
    II. without the state to the person to be served
    III. to a person of suitable age and discretion at the actual dwelling place, business or usual abode of the person to be served
    IV. to a known relative within the stated degree of consanguinity at his actual dwelling place or business
    V. to any person known to the person to be served at his actual dwelling place or business
    The CORRECT answer is:

    A. I, II, III   B. I, III   C. I, III, IV
    D. I, IV, V   E. I, II, III, IV, V

19. When personal service upon a natural person CANNOT be made to the person to be served, or to another suitable person as described by law, service may be made by affixing the summons to the 19.____
    I. door of the actual place of business
    II. door of the actual dwelling place or usual place of abode
    III. windshield of the person's automobile
    IV. door of the last known address
    V. door of the actual place of business or dwelling place of the spouse of the person
    The CORRECT answer is:

    A. I, II   B. I, II, IV   C. I, II, III
    D. II, III, IV   E. I, II, III, IV, V

20. When personal service upon a natural person CANNOT be made to the person to be served, or to a person or place as described by law, service can be made

    A. as the court, upon motion, with notice, directs
    B. as the court, upon motion, without notice, directs
    C. as the court, without notice, directs
    D. as the court, with notice, directs
    E. in any manner deemed fit by the process server

20.____

21. When personal service CANNOT be made in the usual manner prescribed by law, in an action against a natural person based upon nonpayment of any contractual obligation, *additional* notice MUST be given to the defendant by

    A. the court clerk designated in the summons
    B. the county clerk designated in the summons
    C. any authorized public officer
    D. the sheriff designated in the summons
    E. the plaintiff or the attorney for the plaintiff

21.____

22. How many days *prior* to the entry of any default judgment in an action against a natural person based upon nonpayment of any contractual obligation must *additional* notice be given to the defendant who cannot be served in the usual manner?

    A. 3   B. 7   C. 10   D. 15   E. 20

22.____

23. In an action based upon nonpayment of any contractual obligation, when personal service in the usual manner is impractical, notice shall be given to the defendant by mailing a copy of the summons

    A. first class mail to the defendant's last known residence address
    B. registered mail, return receipt requested, to the defendant's last known residence address
    C. certified mail, return receipt requested, to the defendant's last known residence address
    D. express mail to the defendant's last known residence address
    E. insured mail to the defendant's last known residence address

23.____

24. How should an envelope containing a summons unable to be served, be sent to the defendant, in care of his place of employment, be addressed?
    I. "Personal and confidential"
    II. "Official business"
    III. To plaintiff attorney
    IV. With no indication that the communication concerns an alleged debt
    V. To the clerk of court
    The CORRECT answer is:

    A. I, III, IV   B. I, IV   C. I, II, V
    D. II, IV, V   E. I, II

24.____

25. Who should execute an affidavit of any mailing containing a summons unable to be served?

    A. The attorney for the plaintiff
    B. A notary public

25.____

C. The clerk of the court
D. The plaintiff
E. The person mailing the summons

26. An affidavit of any mailing containing a summons unable to be served is filed with the 26.____

    A. clerk of the court
    B. attorney for the plaintiff
    C. judgment
    D. proof of summons
    E. complaint

27. Personal service upon an infant shall be made by personally serving the summons upon 27.____
    I. a parent
    II. a person having legal custody
    III. an adult spouse with whom the infant resides
    IV. any person with whom the infant resides
    V. any person by whom the infant is employed

    The CORRECT answer is:

    A. I, II B. I, II, V C. I, II, IV
    D. I, II, III E. I, II, III, IV, V

28. A summons may be personally served if the infant to be served is at LEAST _____ 28.____
    years old.

    A. 12 B. 14 C. 16 D. 17 E. 18

29. Personal service upon a person judicially declared to be incompetent to manage his 29.____
    affairs shall be made by personally serving

    A. the incompetent
    B. any competent person with knowledge
    C. any competent person known to the incompetent
    D. the committee appointed to manage the incompetent's affairs
    E. all of the above

30. Personal service upon persons conducting a business as a partnership may be made by 30.____
    personally serving the summons upon

    A. any one of them
    B. all of them
    C. the partnership's attorney of record
    D. the partnership's general agent
    E. any employee

31. Personal service upon a corporation shall be made by delivering the summons to a(n) 31.____
    I. officer
    II. director
    III. managing agent
    IV. cashier
    V. adult employee

    The CORRECT answer is:

A. I, II B. I, II, III C. I, II, V
D. I, II, III, IV E. I, II, III, IV, V

32. Personal service upon a city other than New York shall be made by delivering the summons to any of the following EXCEPT the

   A. mayor B. comptroller C. treasurer
   D. clerk E. sheriff

33. Personal service upon a county shall be made by delivering the summons to any of the following EXCEPT the

   A. clerk of the board of supervisors
   B. clerk
   C. trustee
   D. attorney
   E. treasurer

34. Who may be served with the summons WITHOUT the state giving personal jurisdiction? A person

   A. domiciled in the state or subject to the jurisdiction of the state
   B. in a matrimonial action
   C. where levy upon property of the person to be served has been made within the state
   D. where a judgment is demanded that the person to be served be excluded from a vested interest in a specific real property within the state
   E. all of the above

35. Service without the state giving personal jurisdiction may be made by any person authorized to make service

   A. within the state
   B. within the state who is a resident of the state
   C. within and without the state
   D. by the laws of the state in which service is made who is a resident of the state
   E. by federal law

36. Service WITHOUT the state NOT giving personal jurisdiction in a matrimonial action may be made by authorized publication if the

   A. person to be served is not subject to the court of the state
   B. spouse to be served is not subject to the court of the state
   C. person to be served cannot be personally served
   D. judgment involves the custody of infants
   E. service cannot be made by another prescribed method

37. Service of a summons by publication MUST be published in

   A. one newspaper in the language of the person to be served
   B. two newspapers in the language of the person to be served
   C. two newspapers, at least one of which is in the English language
   D. three newspapers, at least one of which is in the English language
   E. all newspapers likely to give notice to the person to served

38. What is the specified time that service of a summons by publication must be published?

    A. Daily for a one week period
    B. Daily for a two week period
    C. At least once in two successive weeks
    D. At least once in each of three successive weeks
    E. At least once in each of four successive weeks

39. Which of the following is NOT required to be published in service of a summons by publication?

    A. The summons
    B. The relief sought
    C. A brief description of real property affected by a judgment
    D. The notice to the defendant
    E. A brief statement of the object of the action

40. What is the specified time that service by a summons by publication in a matrimonial action MUST be published?

    A. Daily for a one week period
    B. Daily for a two week period
    C. At least once in each of two successive weeks
    D. At least once in each of three successive weeks
    E. At least once in each of four successive weeks

41. Service of a summons by publication in a matrimonial action MUST be published in

    A. one newspaper in the English language
    B. one newspaper in the language of the person to be served
    C. two newspapers, one of which is in the English language
    D. two newspapers in the English language
    E. three newspapers, one of which is in the English language

42. The summons in an action for divorce or separation, all orders and papers upon which the order was based shall be filed _____ the first day of publication of service by publication.

    A. 20 days before   B. 10 days before   C. 3 days before
    D. on or before   E. after

43. Within _____ days after the order is granted, the FIRST publication of the summons must be made.

    A. 3   B. 10   C. 20   D. 30   E. 45

44. A person who does not appear and who was served with a summons in a manner other than by personal delivery has _____ after he obtains knowledge of entry of the judgment to defend the action by opening the default.

    A. 30 days   B. 45 days   C. 90 days
    D. 6 months   E. one year

45. A person who does not appear and who was served with a summons in a manner other than by personal delivery has _____ year(s) to defend the action in which he has no knowledge of the entering of the judgment.

   A. 1   B. 5   C. 10   D. 15   E. 20

46. For a person to defend an action in which he did not appear by service in a manner other than by personal delivery, it is necessary

   A. to appear before the court
   B. to appear before the court in a specified time period
   C. to appear before the court after obtaining knowledge of the judgment
   D. to appear before the court in time to defend and show a meritorious defense
   E. there is no condition to defend

47. How long is the designation of agent for service in effect after filing?

   A. 1 year
   B. 3 years
   C. 5 years
   D. 10 years
   E. until it is revoked by action or death of either party

48. A designation of agent for service is filed in the office of the

   A. clerk of the county in which the principal to be served resides or has his principal office
   B. clerk of the county in which the designated agent of the principal to be served resides or has his principal office
   C. court designated by the summons
   D. county clerk that is the designated venue specified in the summons
   E. attorney of record for the principal to be served

49. A person may be designated by a natural person as an agent for service in a writing

   A. with the consent of the agent endorsed thereon
   B. with the consent of the court
   C. certified by a notary public
   D. acknowledging that a substantial right of the party for whom the summons is issued is not prejudiced
   E. acknowledging that a substantial right of the designated agent is not prejudiced

50. Personal service upon a town may be made by delivering the summons to the

   A. comptroller   B. sheriff   C. mayor
   D. supervisor   E. trustee

KEY (CORRECT ANSWERS)

1.	C	11.	C	21.	E	31.	D	41.	A
2.	E	12.	A	22.	E	32.	E	42.	D
3.	A	13.	C	23.	A	33.	C	43.	C
4.	D	14.	D	24.	B	34.	A	44.	E
5.	E	15.	D	25.	E	35.	B	45.	B
6.	B	16.	E	26.	C	36.	E	46.	D
7.	D	17.	C	27.	E	37.	C	47.	B
8.	B	18.	B	28.	B	38.	E	48.	A
9.	D	19.	A	29.	D	39.	B	49.	A
10.	A	20.	B	30.	A	40.	D	50.	D

EXAMINATION SECTION
TEST 1

DIRECTIONS: Each question or incomplete statement is followed by several suggested answers or completions. Select the one that BEST answers the question or completes the statement. *PRINT THE LETTER OF THE CORRECT ANSWER IN THE SPACE AT THE RIGHT.*

1. The rules contained in the Civil Practice Law and Rules (CPLR) MAY be amended ONLY by the
    I. Appellate Divisions
    II. Judicial Conference
    III. Legislature
    IV. Court of Appeals
   The CORRECT answer is:

   A. I only   B. II only   C. I, IV   D. II, III

2. The procedure in civil judicial proceedings in all courts of the state is

   A. governed by the CPLR unless the procedure is regulated by an inconsistent statute
   B. governed by the CPLR when there is an inconsistent statute
   C. governed by the Civil Practice Act
   D. always governed by the CPLR

3. Which of the following statements is(are) CORRECT?
    I. Procedural requirements under the CPLR should be strictly construed.
    II. The words *special proceeding* include an action.
    III. Except where otherwise prescribed by law, procedure in special proceedings shall be the same as in actions.
    IV. If a court has obtained jurisdiction over the parties, a civil judicial proceeding can still be dismissed SOLELY because it is not brought in the proper form.
    V. Under the CPLR, the word *judgment* means only a final judgment.
   The CORRECT answer is:

   A. I, II, III, IV, V   B. I, II, III, IV
   C. I, II, IV, V   D. III only

4. Which of the following are CORRECT?
   The person prosecuting a civil action or proceeding may be called
    I. petitioner
    II. poor person
    III. plaintiff
    IV. respondent
    V. defendant
   The CORRECT answer is:

   A. I, II, III   B. II, III, V   C. IV, V   D. II, III

5. A special proceeding may BEST be described as

   A. an important civil judicial proceeding
   B. a civil judicial proceeding wherein prosecution in the form of a special proceeding is authorized
   C. all civil judicial proceedings which are not designated *actions* in the CPLR
   D. a civil judicial proceeding relating solely to election matters

6. A civil action is commenced by the service of a

   A. subpoena
   B. subpoena duces tecum
   C. summons
   D. complaint

7. Which of the following, if any, are necessary parties who MUST be joined in an action?
   Persons
   I. who ought to be parties if complete relief is to be accorded between the parties who are parties to the action
   II. who assert a right of joint relief arising out of the same transaction involved in the complaint where there is a common question of law or of fact
   III. designated by the court in an order to show cause
   IV. who, if not joined, might be inequitably affected by a judgment
   The CORRECT answer is:

   A. None of the above
   B. All of the above
   C. II, III
   D. I, IV

8. Which of the following statements is(are) INCORRECT?
   I. The difference between permissive joinder and necessary joinder is that permissive joinder means that parties may be joined in an action only when they consent.
   II. An action may continue without joinder of necessary parties but only by permission of the court when justice requires and when jurisdiction cannot be obtained over the necessary party except by his consent or appearance.
   III. When a person who should be a plaintiff refuses to join the action, he may be made a third-party defendant.
   IV. When a person who should be a plaintiff refuses to join the action as such, he may be made a defendant.
   V. An action may never continue without joinder of necessary parties.
   The CORRECT answer is:

   A. V *only*
   B. I, II, IV
   C. II, IV
   D. I, III, V

9. In determining whether to permit an action to proceed without the joinder of a necessary party, the court should consider whether
   I. the guardian of an infant may be made a party
   II. jurisdiction may be obtained by substituted service
   III. the plaintiff has an effective remedy in case the action is dismissed on account of the nonjoinder
   IV. an effective judgment may be rendered in the absence of a person who is not joined
   The CORRECT answer is:

   A. I, II, III
   B. II, III, IV
   C. I, II
   D. III, IV

10. Which of the following statements is (are) INCORRECT?
    I. Misjoinder of parties may be a ground for dismissal of an action.
    II. The court may order the addition or deletion of a party only on a motion by one of the parties.
    III. A guardian of an infant's property may be sued without joining the infant as a party.
    IV. An action may never be dismissed for nonjoinder of a necessary party.
    The CORRECT answer is:

    E. III only F. I, II G. I, II, III H. I, II, III, IV

11. An action in which there is a common question of interest to many persons may be brought in the form of a(n)

    A. motion for leave to intervene
    B. successive third-party complaint
    C. class action
    D. interpleader action

12. Which of the following statements, if any, is(are) INCORRECT?
    I. The Attorney-General must be notified by the court when the constitutionality of a state statute is involved in the action.
    II. The Attorney-General may be permitted to intervene in the discretion of the court when public retirement benefits are at issue.
    III. A person shall be permitted to intervene as of right when the representation of that person's interest by the parties already in the action may be inadequate provided a timely motion is made.
    IV. A person shall be permitted to intervene in an action as of right at any time prior to final judgment.
    The CORRECT answer is:

    A. I, III B. I only C. II, III D. II, IV

13. Which of the following statements, if any, is(are) INCORRECT?
    I. The stakeholder may be discharged of his liability for a liquidated claim by conceding the liability and paying the fund or the object of the claim into court.
    II. Interpleader is a procedure whereby a person who is called a stakeholder may be brought into an action in which there are adverse claimants to the same fund.
    III. Intervention is a procedure whereby a person who is called a stakeholder may be brought into an action in which there are adverse claimants to the same fund.
    IV. Intervention is a procedure by which a person not a party to an action enters that action for the purpose of protecting his rights.
    The CORRECT answer is:

    A. I, IV B. II only C. I only D. II, III

14. John Doe has been held in contempt for his refusal to call off an illegal strike against his employer. Doe has been arrested and is lodged in the civil jail.
    Doe may be kept in jail

    A. not more than three months
    B. not more than six months
    C. until he posts bail
    D. until he calls off the strike

15. In executing an order of civil arrest, the LEAST desirable place to make the arrest is

    A. the defendant's place of business
    B. in a public place
    C. on the street outside the defendant's home
    D. the defendant's home

16. An order of civil arrest has been issued for an Orthodox Jew.
    On which of the following days is he immune from arrest?

    A. Only on Saturday
    B. Only on Sunday
    C. On both Saturday and Sunday
    D. Neither on Saturday nor on Sunday

17. Of the following persons, the one who is NOT immune from civil arrest is a(n)

    A. ordained clergyman
    B. maid who works at the French Ambassador's home
    C. fireman on duty
    D. marine on active duty

18. After an order of civil arrest has been signed, it

    A. may not be withdrawn without a court order
    B. must be executed within ten days
    C. must be filed in the county clerk's office
    D. may be withdrawn by the plaintiff's attorney anytime before it is executed

19. Even though the defendant is known to be in New York, the one of the following which need NOT be personally served upon him is a(n)

    A. order preliminarily enjoining the defendant
    B. order temporarily restraining the defendant
    C. subpoena duces tecum commanding defendant to deliver books
    D. summons

20. The provisional remedy of civil arrest is available in an action for

    A. trespass to a chattel
    B. ejectment
    C. specific performance of a contract to convey land located outside the state
    D. specific performance of a contract to convey land located in the state

KEY (CORRECT ANSWERS)

1.	D	11.	C
2.	A	12.	D
3.	D	13.	D
4.	A	14.	D
5.	B	15.	D
6.	C	16.	C
7.	D	17.	A
8.	D	18.	D
9.	D	19.	A
10.	C	20.	C

TEST 2

DIRECTIONS: Each question or incomplete statement is followed by several suggested answers or completions. Select the one that BEST answers the question or completes the statement. *PRINT THE LETTER OF THE CORRECT ANSWER IN THE SPACE AT THE RIGHT.*

1. The FIRST paper served in a civil action in the Supreme Court is a

    A. subpoena   B. injunction   C. summons   D. complaint

2. The books containing the decisions of the New York courts are known as

    A. framed issues   B. citations
    C. reports   D. references

3. The term applied to a person appointed to represent an infant in an action in the Supreme Court is:

    A. Testamentary guardian   B. Guardian ad litem
    C. Referee   D. Guardian of the person

4. The statute of limitations is a law limiting the

    A. sentence that may be imposed upon conviction for a particular crime
    B. courts in which an action may be brought
    C. amount of money that may be awarded in a civil action
    D. time within which criminal prosecution or civil action must be commenced

5. A guardian ad litem is a guardian for

    A. the purpose of conserving real property
    B. the purpose of representing a corporation
    C. a particular lawsuit
    D. all purposes

6. In an ex parte proceeding,

    A. special relief is sought by both parties in judge's chambers
    B. only one side is heard without notice to the other side
    C. each side is heard separately before the court on different days
    D. both sides are heard before a court without a jury

7. 29 N.Y.S. 2d 53 means, in part,

    A. 53rd volume   B. 29th page
    C. second volume   D. 2d series

8. When a court refers to *McKinney's,* it means the

    A. rules of evidence
    B. local ordinances
    C. consolidated laws of New York State
    D. federal rules

9. A poor person is a(n)

    A. infant whose father has less than $300 in property
    B. person who has been adjudicated an incompetent
    C. person who is unable to pay the costs, fees, and expenses necessary to prosecute or defend the action
    D. person who has less than $300 in real or personal property

10. Which of the following statements are CORRECT?
    I. A motion for the appointment of a guardian ad litem may be made at any stage of the action.
    II. The court may direct the appearance of an adult who is incapable of adequately prosecuting or defending his rights by a guardian ad litem even if that adult has not been judicially declared incompetent.
    III. An infant must always appear in an action by a guardian ad litem.
    IV. Where an infant is over 14 years of age, it is not necessary to serve a copy of a notice of motion for the appointment of a guardian ad litem on anyone other than the infant.
    V. A default judgment may never be entered against an infant or a person judicially declared to be an incompetent.
    VI. A controversy involving an adult incapable of adequately protecting his rights may be submitted to arbitration without a court order.

    The CORRECT answer is:

    A. I, IV, V   B. I, II, III   C. I, II, IV   D. I, II, VI

11. New York courts do NOT acquire jurisdiction over a nonresident under the *long-arm* statute when the cause of action arises out of

    A. the commission of a tort in New York
    B. solicitation of business within New York by the circulation of catalogues
    C. entering into a contract in New York
    D. possession of real property in New York

12. An article 78 proceeding may be brought against a public official or body

    A. to review capricious acts
    B. to enjoin such a body from proceeding where it is claimed that the action is unauthorized
    C. to compel the performance of a duty required by law
    D. for all of the above

13. A motion for summary judgment in lieu of a complaint is available in an action

    A. on account stated
    B. to recover payments pursuant to a separation agreement
    C. other than a matrimonial action if the moving papers establish a prima facie case and there is no real defense
    D. based upon a judgment

14. In which of the following provisional remedies, granted before a summons is served, must jurisdiction be acquired over the defendant or his property within a certain time limit or else the provisional remedy becomes void?
Attachment

    A. and arrest
    B. and lis pendens (notice of pendency)
    C. arrest, and receivership
    D. injunction, and lis pendens (notice of pendency)

15. The sheriff has properly delivered an income execution to D's employer. The employer has refused to honor the execution.
The plaintiff's lawyer should NOW serve

    A. motion papers on the employer to punish him for contempt
    B. a notice of petition and a petition to obtain a judgment against the employer
    C. motion papers on the employer, to obtain an order directing payment
    D. a subpoena upon the employer restraining him from paying D

16. An order of civil arrest has been signed against Doe in an action for fraud. The action has not yet been commenced.
The summons MUST be served

    A. within 48 hours after Doe is arrested
    B. within 30 days after the arrest order is signed or the arrest order will become void
    C. at the time the deputy sheriff arrests Doe
    D. at a time not specified by any of the foregoing

17. The date on which a summons is prepared in a civil action

    A. is the date upon which the statute of limitations stops running
    B. is the date from which the defendant measures his time in which to appear
    C. must be typed on the face of the summons
    D. has no legal significance

18. An attorney has delivered an execution to the sheriff's office.
A levy may thereafter be made under this execution within sixty days

    A. or else the execution becomes void and cannot be extended
    B. unless the period is extended (by a maximum of one sixty-day increment) in writing by the plaintiff's attorney
    C. unless the period is extended by court order
    D. unless the period is extended by successive sixty-day periods in writing by the plaintiff's attorney

19. John Doe, a judgment debtor, has personal property stored in a warehouse owned by X. X has issued to Doe a negotiable warehouse receipt for the property.
A PROPER way to levy upon this property is to

    A. go to the warehouse and seize the property
    B. seize the warehouse receipt from Doe
    C. go to the warehouse and leave the execution with X
    D. do none of the foregoing

20. A and B, two individuals, are partners in a finance company known as Ace Finance. A judgment has been entered against B for his negligence in driving his family automobile on a pleasure trip to Miami.
   This judgment may be executed by levying upon

   A. B's desk in the office of Ace Finance
   B. B's interest in the partnership
   C. a bank account maintained in the name of Ace Finance
   D. B's Timex watch, worth $25.00

20.____

KEY (CORRECT ANSWERS)

1. C
2. C
3. B
4. D
5. C

6. B
7. D
8. C
9. C
10. D

11. B
12. D
13. D
14. B
15. B

16. C
17. D
18. D
19. B
20. B

TEST 3

DIRECTIONS: Each question or incomplete statement is followed by several suggested answers or completions. Select the one that BEST answers the question or completes the statement. *PRINT THE LETTER OF TEE CORRECT ANSWER IN THE SPACE AT THE RIGHT.*

1. Escheat is a legal term meaning that

    A. a fraud has been committed
    B. property has reverted to the state
    C. an agent's license has been revoked
    D. property under a trust deed may be reconveyed

2. A contract of sale passes

    A. the full fee simple title to the purchaser
    B. only an equitable title
    C. the legal title
    D. an estate for years

3. The instrument used to remove the lien of a trust deed from record is called a

    A. satisfaction
    B. release
    C. deed of reconveyance
    D. certificate of redemption

4. A power of attorney is terminated by

    A. an express revocation by the principal
    B. the death of the principal
    C. incapability of the principal to contract
    D. any of the above

5. For negotiating the sale of a business opportunity business without a license, a person may be prosecuted by a(n)

    A. jury
    B. judge of a superior court
    C. district attorney
    D. attorney general

6. A married woman is legally capable of contracting at the minimum age of

    A. seventeen B. eighteen C. twenty D. twenty-one

7. In searching the records at the county recorder's office, you can usually distinguish a second trust deed from the first trust deed by the

    A. heading of the recorded documents
    B. information contained in the note
    C. recorder's declaration
    D. time and date of recordation

8. The MINIMUM time which must run after publication of a notice to creditors, under the provisions of the Uniform Commercial Code pertaining to bulk sales before consummation of the sale, is _____ days.

    A. 5 B. 10 C. 15 D. 20

9. To be valid, a bill of sale MUST be

   A. dated B. signed C. notarized D. witnessed

10. Property held in joint tenancy, upon the death of one of the tenants, passes to the

    A. landlord
    B. state
    C. county assessor
    D. surviving joint tenant

11. Alienation expresses a meaning MOST completely opposite to

    A. acquisition
    B. ad valorem
    C. acceleration
    D. amortization

12. Anything that is fastened or attached to real property permanently is considered to be _____ property.

    A. personal B. real C. private D. separate

13. The instrument used to secure a loan on personal property is called a

    A. bill of sale
    B. trust deed
    C. security agreement
    D. bill of exchange

14. A promissory note that provides for payment of interest only during the term of the note would be a(n) _____ note.

    A. installment
    B. straight
    C. amortized
    D. non-negotiable

15. Community property is property owned by

    A. churches
    B. husband and wife
    C. the municipality
    D. the community

16. The seller is sometimes called the

    A. vendee B. vendor C. lessee D. lessor

17. A contract based on an illegal consideration is

    A. valid B. void C. legal D. enforceable

18. A check that has been altered or raised by a person other than the maker is

    A. valid B. invalid C. cancelled D. dishonorable

19. A valid bill of sale MUST contain

    A. a date
    B. an acknowledgment
    C. the seller's signature
    D. a verification

20. A security agreement is USUALLY given in connection with

    A. real property
    B. agricultural property
    C. rentals
    D. personal property

21. Title to fixtures, shelves, counters, and merchandise is transferred or conveyed by

    A. deed
    B. bill of sale
    C. security agreement
    D. escrow

22. Involuntary alienation of an estate means:

    A. Estate cannot be transferred without the consent of the owner
    B. Aliens are forbidden to own estates in fee simple in the state
    C. Ownership of estates may be transferred by operation of law
    D. No one can be compelled to transfer title without his consent

23. When a broker receives a deposit on a business which he has listed, the money becomes the property of the

    A. seller
    B. broker
    C. escrow company
    D. prospective buyers

24. A financing statement may be released from the records by

    A. payment in full
    B. a reconveyance
    C. filing a release statement
    D. death of the mortgagor

25. The stock and fixtures that are to be transferred with the sale of a business are usually enumerated in a(n)

    A. contract of sale
    B. inventory
    C. deed
    D. appraisal

KEY (CORRECT ANSWERS)

1. B	11. A
2. C	12. B
3. A	13. C
4. D	14. B
5. C	15. B
6. B	16. B
7. B	17. B
8. A	18. B
9. B	19. C
10. D	20. D

21. A
22. C
23. A
24. A
25. B

EXAMINATION SECTION
TEST 1

DIRECTIONS: Each question or incomplete statement is followed by several suggested answers or completions. Select the one that BEST answers the question or completes the statement. *PRINT THE LETTER OF THE CORRECT ANSWER IN THE SPACE AT THE RIGHT.*

Questions 1-50.

DIRECTIONS: Each of Questions 1 through 50 consists of a word in capital letters followed by four suggested meanings of the word. For each question, choose the word or phrase which means MOST NEARLY the same as the word in capital letters.

1. ABUT
   A. abandon   B. assist   C. border on   D. renounce

   1.____

2. ABSCOND
   A. draw in   B. give up
   C. refrain from   D. deal off

   2.____

3. BEQUEATH
   A. deaden   B. hand down   C. make sad   D. scold

   3.____

4. BOGUS
   A. sad   B. false   C. shocking   D. stolen

   4.____

5. CALAMITY
   A. disaster   B. female   C. insanity   D. patriot

   5.____

6. COMPULSORY
   A. binding   B. ordinary   C. protected   D. ruling

   6.____

7. CONSIGN
   A. agree with   B. benefit
   C. commit   D. drive down

   7.____

8. DEBILITY
   A. failure   B. legality
   C. quality   D. weakness

   8.____

9. DEFRAUD
   A. cheat   B. deny
   C. reveal   D. tie

   9.____

10. DEPOSITION
    A. absence   B. publication
    C. removal   D. testimony

    10.____

11. DOMICILE
    A. anger   B. dwelling
    C. tame   D. willing

    11.____

23

12. HEARSAY
   A. selfish   B. serious   C. rumor   D. unlikely   12.___

13. HOMOGENEOUS
   A. human   B. racial   C. similar   D. unwise   13.___

14. ILLICIT
   A. understood   B. uneven   C. unkind   D. unlawful   14.___

15. LEDGER
   A. book of accounts   B. editor
   C. periodical   D. shelf   15.___

16. NARRATIVE
   A. gossip   B. natural   C. negative   D. story   16.___

17. PLAUSIBLE
   A. reasonable   B. respectful   C. responsible   D. rightful   17.___

18. RECIPIENT
   A. absentee   B. receiver   C. speaker   D. substitute   18.___

19. SUBSTANTIATE
   A. appear for   B. arrange
   C. confirm   D. combine   19.___

20. SURMISE
   A. aim   B. break   C. guess   D. order   20.___

21. ALTER EGO
   A. business partner   B. confidential friend
   C. guide   D. subconscious conflict   21.___

22. FOURTH ESTATE
   A. the aristocracy   B. the clergy
   C. the judiciary   D. the newspapers   22.___

23. IMPEACH
   A. accuse   B. find guilty
   C. remove   D. try   23.___

24. PROPENSITY
   A. dislike   B. helpfulness
   C. inclination   D. supervision   24.___

25. SPLENETIC
   A. charming   B. peevish   C. shining   D. sluggish   25.___

26. SUBORN
   A. bribe someone to commit perjury
   B. demote someone several levels in rank
   C. deride
   D. substitute   26.___

27. TALISMAN
    A. charm
    B. juror
    C. prayer shawl
    D. native

28. VITREOUS
    A. corroding
    B. glassy
    C. nourishing
    D. sticky

29. WRY
    A. comic
    B. grained
    C. resilient
    D. twisted

30. SIGNATORY
    A. lawyer who draws up a legal document
    B. document that must be signed by a judge
    C. person who signs a document
    D. true copy of a signature

31. RETAINER
    A. fee paid to a lawyer for his services
    B. document held by a third party
    C. court decision to send a prisoner back to custody pending trial
    D. legal requirement to keep certain types of files

32. BEQUEATH
    A. to receive assistance from a charitable organization
    B. to give personal property by will to another
    C. to transfer real property from one person to another
    D. to receive an inheritance upon the death of a relative

33. RATIFY
    A. approve and sanction
    B. forego
    C. produce evidence
    D. summarize

34. CODICIL
    A. document introduced in evidence in a civil action
    B. subsection of a law
    C. type of legal action that can be brought by a plaintiff
    D. supplement or an addition to a will

35. ALIAS
    A. assumed name
    B. in favor of
    C. against
    D. a writ

36. PROXY
    A. a phony document in a real estate transaction
    B. an opinion by a judge of a civil court
    C. a document containing appointment of an agent
    D. a summons in a lawsuit

37. ALLEGED
    A. innocent
    B. asserted
    C. guilty
    D. called upon

38. EXECUTE
    A. to complete a legal document by signing it
    B. to set requirements
    C. to render services to a duly elected executive of a municipality
    D. to initiate legal action such as a lawsuit

39. NOTARY PUBLIC
    A. lawyer who is running for public office
    B. judge who hears minor cases
    C. public officer, one of whose functions is to administer oaths
    D. lawyer who gives free legal services to persons unable to pay

40. WAIVE
    A. to disturb a calm state of affairs
    B. to knowingly renounce a right or claim
    C. to pardon someone for a minor fault
    D. to purposely mislead a person during an investigation

41. ARRAIGN
    A. to prevent an escape
    B. to defend a prisoner
    C. to verify a document
    D. to accuse in a court of law

42. VOLUNTARY
    A. by free choice   B. necessary
    C. important   D. by design

43. INJUNCTION
    A. act of prohibiting   B. process of inserting
    C. means of arbitrating   D. freedom of action

44. AMICABLE
    A. compelled   B. friendly
    C. unimportant   D. insignificant

45. CLOSED SHOP
    A. one that employs only members of a union
    B. one that employs union members and unaffiliated employees
    C. one that employs only employees with previous experience
    D. one that employs skilled and unskilled workers

46. ABDUCT
    A. lead   B. kidnap   C. sudden   D. worthless

47. BIAS
    A. ability   B. envy   C. prejudice D. privilege

48. COERCE
    A. cancel   B. force   C. rescind   D. rugged

49. CONDONE
    A. combine   B. pardon   C. revive   D. spice

50. CONSISTENCY
    A. bravery   B. readiness
    C. strain   D. uniformity

KEY (CORRECT ANSWERS)

1. C	11. B	21. B	31. A	41. D
2. D	12. C	22. D	32. B	42. A
3. B	13. C	23. A	33. A	43. A
4. B	14. D	24. C	34. D	44. B
5. A	15. A	25. B	35. A	45. A
6. A	16. D	26. A	36. C	46. B
7. C	17. A	27. A	37. B	47. C
8. D	18. B	28. B	38. A	48. B
9. A	19. C	29. D	39. C	49. B
10. D	20. C	30. C	40. B	50. D

TEST 2

DIRECTIONS: Each question or incomplete statement is followed by several suggested answers or completions. Select the one that BEST answers the question or completes the statement. *PRINT THE LETTER OF THE CORRECT ANSWER IN THE SPACE AT THE RIGHT.*

1. In the sentence, *The prisoner was fractious when brought to the station house*, the word *fractious* means MOST NEARLY
    A. penitent
    B. talkative
    C. irascible
    D. broken-hearted

2. In the sentence, *The judge was implacable when the attorney pleaded for leniency*, the word *implacable* means MOST NEARLY
    A. inexorable
    B. disinterested
    C. inattentive
    D. indifferent

3. In the sentence, *The court ordered the mendacious statements stricken from the record*, the word *mendacious* means MOST NEARLY
    A. begging
    B. lying
    C. threatening
    D. lengthy

4. In the sentence, *The district attorney spoke in a strident voice*, the word *strident* means MOST NEARLY
    A. loud
    B. harsh-sounding
    C. sing-song
    D. low

5. In the sentence, *The speaker had a predilection for long sentences*, the word *predilection* means MOST NEARLY
    A. aversion
    B. talent
    C. propensity
    D. diffidence

6. A person who has an uncontrollable desire to steal without need is called a
    A. dipsomaniac
    B. kleptomaniac
    C. monomaniac
    D. pyromaniac

7. In the sentence, *Malice was immanent in all his remarks*, the word *immanent* means MOST NEARLY
    A. elevated
    B. inherent
    C. threatening
    D. foreign

8. In the sentence, *The extant copies of the document were found in the safe*, the word *extant* means MOST NEARLY
    A. existing
    B. original
    C. forged
    D. duplicate

9. In the sentence, *The recruit was more complaisant after the captain spoke to him*, the word *complaisant* means MOST NEARLY
    A. calm
    B. affable
    C. irritable
    D. confident

10. In the sentence, *The man was captured under highly creditable circumstances*, the word *creditable* means MOST NEARLY
    A. doubtful
    B. believable
    C. praiseworthy
    D. unexpected

11. In the sentence, *His superior officers were more sagacious than he*, the word *sagacious* means MOST NEARLY
    A. shrewd
    B. obtuse
    C. absurd
    D. verbose

12. In the sentence, *He spoke with impunity*, the word *impunity* means MOST NEARLY
    A. rashness
    B. caution
    C. without fear
    D. immunity

13. In the sentence, *The new officer displayed unusual temerity during the emergency*, the word *temerity* means MOST NEARLY
    A. fear
    B. rashness
    C. calmness
    D. anxiety

14. In the sentence, *The portions of food were parsimoniously served*, the word *parsimoniously* means MOST NEARLY
    A. stingily
    B. piously
    C. elaborately
    D. generously

15. In the sentence, *Generally the speaker's remarks were sententious*, the word *sententious* means MOST NEARLY
    A. verbose
    B. witty
    C. argumentative
    D. pithy

Questions 16-20.

DIRECTIONS: Next to the number which corresponds with the number of each item in Column I, place the letter preceding the adjective in Column II which BEST describes the persons in Column I.

COLUMN I	COLUMN II
16. Talkative woman	A. abstemious
17. Person on a reducing diet	B. pompous
18. Scholarly professor	C. erudite
19. Man who seldom speaks	D. benevolent
20. Charitable person	E. docile
	F. loquacious
	G. indefatigable
	H. taciturn

Questions 21-25.

DIRECTIONS: Next to the number which corresponds with the number preceding each profession in Column I, place the letter preceding the word in Column II which BEST explains the subject matter of that profession.

COLUMN I	COLUMN II	
21. Geologist	A. animals	21.__
22. Oculist	B. eyes	22.__
23. Podiatrist	C. feet	23.__
24. Palmist	D. fortune-telling	24.__
25. Zoologist	E. language	25.__
	F. rocks	
	G. stamps	
	H. woman	

Questions 26-30.

DIRECTIONS: Next to the number corresponding to the number of each of the words in Column I, place the letter preceding the word in Column II that is MOST NEARLY OPPOSITE to it in meaning.

COLUMN I	COLUMN II	
26. comely	A. beautiful	26.__
27. eminent	B. cowardly	27.__
28. frugal	C. kind	28.__
29. gullible	D. sedate	29.__
30. valiant	E. shrewd	30.__
	F. ugly	
	G. unknown	
	H. wasteful	

KEY (CORRECT ANSWERS)

1. C
2. A
3. B
4. B
5. C
6. B
7. B
8. A
9. B
10. C
11. A
12. D
13. B
14. A
15. D
16. F
17. A
18. C
19. H
20. D
21. F
22. B
23. C
24. D
25. A
26. F
27. G
28. H
29. E
30. B

VISUAL SCANNING
MAP READING

COMMENTARY

This is a test of your ability to orient yourself within a given section or neighborhood of a city or community. In each problem, you are in a vehicle, and you are to choose the shortest way to get from one location to another without breaking any laws. In order to solve each problem, you will need to study the map accompanying each set of four problems. Always begin with the first problem in the set. The starting point for the vehicle in the first problem will be marked by the symbol ➡. On the sample map below, the vehicle is heading east on Scott. You will be asked to find your way from the first location to the second location. Each location will be marked with an X. Some of the streets on the map are one-way streets. An arrow ⇨ shows the direction in which you may travel on a street. If there is no arrow, you may travel in either direction. These maps are NOT real. Do not confuse them with any area you may know. Below is a sample problem

SAMPLE QUESTION

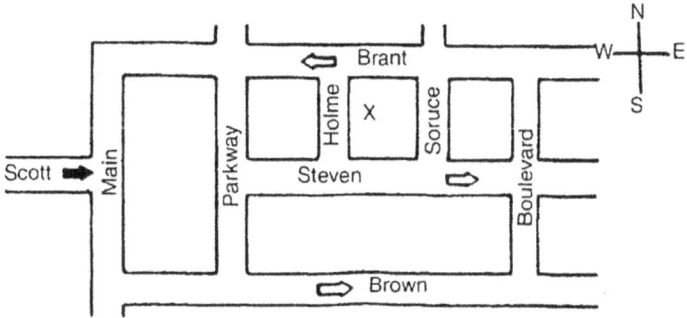

You are on Scott, and you are going to Holme. What is the MOST direct way to get there without breaking the law?
You are on Scott, and you are going to Holme. What is the MOST direct way to get there without breaking the law?

    A. Go right on Main, left on Brown, left on Boulevard, left on Steven, right on Holme to telephone
    B. Go left on Main, right on Brant, right on Holme to telephone
    C. Go right on Main, left on Brown, left on Parkway, right on Steven, left on Holme to telephone
    D. Go right on Main, left on Brown, left on Boulevard, left on Brant, left on Holme to telephone

The MOST direct way to get from the starting point to the location without breaking the law is described in choice C. Therefore, you would have marked C in the space at the right.

EXAMINATION SECTION
TEST 1

DIRECTIONS: Each map will be followed by several questions. For each question, you will be asked to go from one street to another street. There is ONLY ONE viable selection for each question, although it may not be the shortest route. Any street marked with either a ➡ or a ⬅ is a one-way street. Unmarked streets are two-ways.
In some cases, a PARTICULAR location on a street is mentioned in the question. This information should be used in arriving at a correct answer. All maps are hypothetical. *PRINT THE LETTER OF THE CORRECT ANSWER IN THE SPACE AT THE RIGHT.*

Questions 1-5.

DIRECTIONS: For Questions 1 to 5, use the following map.

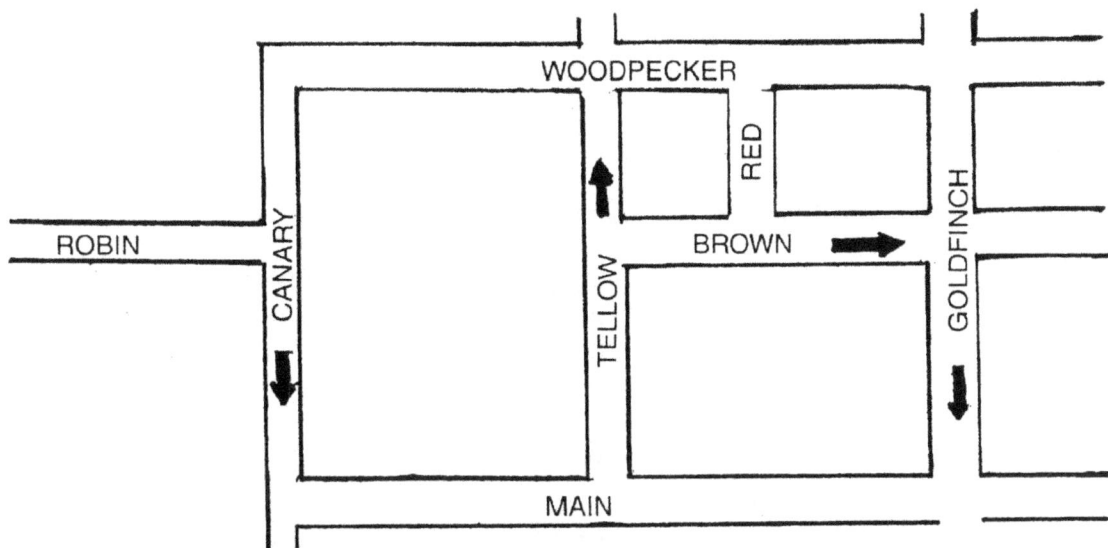

1. From Brown (east of Red) to Robin.

    A. Left on Goldfinch, left on Woodpecker, left on Canary, right on Robin
    B. Right on Goldfinch, right on Main, right on Yellow, left on Woodpecker, left on Canary, right on Robin
    C. Right on Goldfinch, right on Main, right on Canary, left on Robin
    D. Right on Goldfinch, left on Main, right on Canary, right on Robin

1.____

2. From Canary to Red.

    A. Left on Main, left on Goldfinch, left on Woodpecker, left on Red
    B. Left on Main, left on Yellow, left on Woodpecker, right on Red
    C. Left on Main, left on Yellow, right on Brown, left on Red
    D. Right on Main, left on Goldfinch, left on Brown, right on Red

2.____

3. From Woodpecker (west of Yellow) to Brown.　　　　　　　　　　　　　　　3.___

   A. Left on Canary, left on Main, left on Yellow, right on Robin
   B. Right on Yellow, left on Brown
   C. Right on Yellow, left on Main, left on Goldfinch, right on Brown
   D. Right on Goldfinch, left on Brown

4. From Robin to Goldfinch.　　　　　　　　　　　　　　　4.___

   A. Right on Canary, left on Main, left on Goldfinch
   B. Left on Canary, right on Woodpecker, right on Goldfinch
   C. Right on Canary, left on Main, left on Yellow, right on Brown, right on Goldfinch
   D. Right on Canary, left on Main, right on Yellow, left on Brown, left on Goldfinch

5. From Red to Main.　　　　　　　　　　　　　　　5.___

   A. Left on Brown, left on Goldfinch, left on Main
   B. Right on Brown, right on Yellow, left on Woodpecker, right on Canary, left on Main
   C. Right on Brown, left on Yellow, right on Main
   D. Left on Brown, right on Goldfinch, right on Main

Questions 6-11.

DIRECTIONS: For Questions 6 to 11, use the following map.

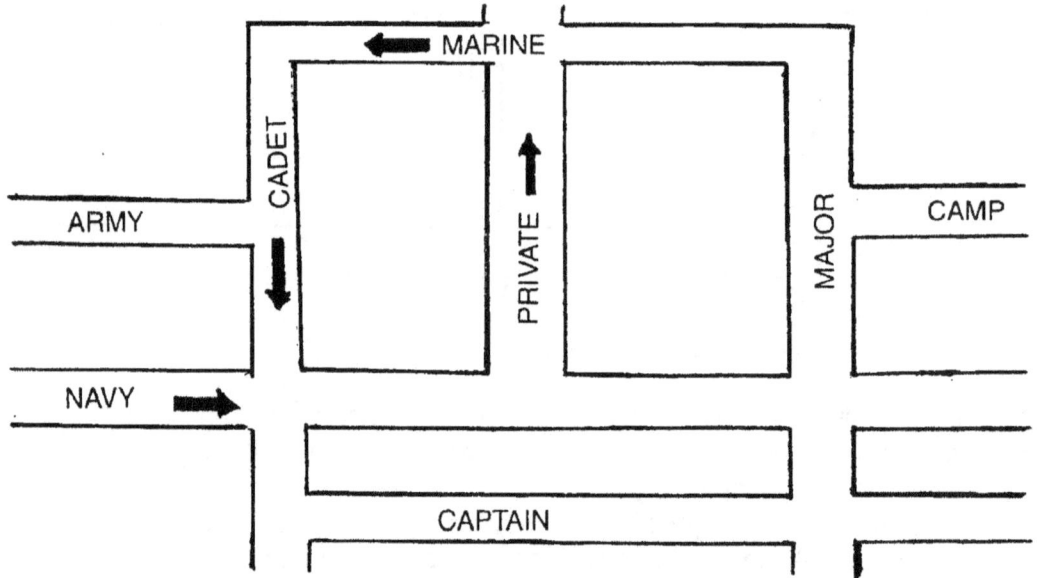

6. From Army to Camp.　　　　　　　　　　　　　　　6.___

   A. Right on Cadet, left on Navy, right on Major, right on Camp
   B. Left on Cadet, left on Marine, right on Major, left on Camp
   C. Right on Cadet, left on Navy, left on Major, right on Camp
   D. Right on Cadet, right on Navy, left on Major, left on Camp

7. From Captain to Marine.　　　　　　　　　　　　　　　7.___

   A. Left on Major, left on Marine
   B. Left on Major, left on Navy, right on Private, left on Marine

36

C. Right on Cadet, right on Marine
D. Right on Cadet, right on Navy, left on Private, left on Marine

8. From Navy (between Private and Major) to Cadet. 8._____

   A. Right on Major, right on Captain, right on Cadet
   B. Right on Private, left on Marine, right on Cadet
   C. Left on Major, left on Marine, left on Cadet
   D. Right on Captain, right on Navy, right on Cadet

9. From Navy (west of Cadet) to Array. 9._____

   A. Left on Private, left on Marine, left on Cadet, right on Army
   B. Left on Private, right on Marine, right on Army
   C. Left on Cadet, left on Army
   D. Right on Major, right on Captain, right on Cadet, left on Army

10. From Major to Army. 10._____

    A. Right on Navy, right on Cadet, right on Army
    B. Right on Captain, right on Cadet, left on Army
    C. Right on Navy, right on Private, left on Marine left on Cadet, right on Army
    D. Left on Marine, left on Cadet, right on Army

11. From Private to Captain. 11._____

    A. Right on Marine, right on Major, right on Captain
    B. Left on Navy, left on Major, right on Captain
    C. Left on Marine, left on Cadet, left on Captain
    D. Left on Marine, left on Cadet, left on Navy, left on Major, right on Captain

Questions 12-18.

DIRECTIONS: For Questions 12 to 18, use the following map.

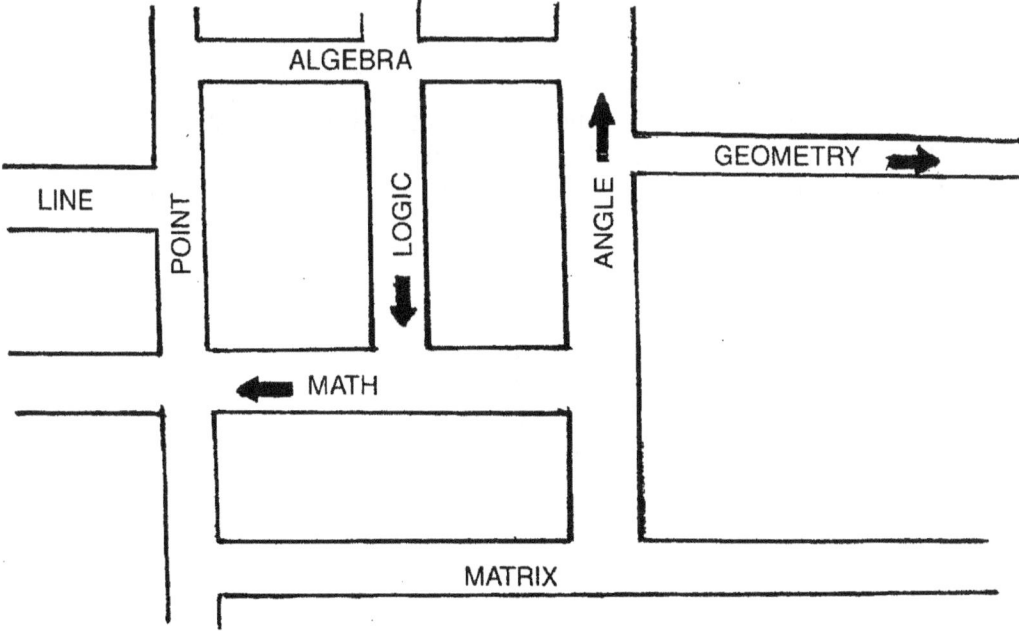

12. From Math to Angle (north of Algebra). 12.____
    A. Left on Point, right on Matrix, left on Angle
    B. Right on Point, right on Algebra, left on Angle
    C. Right on Logic, right on Algebra, left on Angle
    D. Left on Logic, left on Matrix, left on Angle

13. From Algebra to Geometry. 13.____
    A. Left on Logic, left on Math, right on Angle, right on Geometry
    B. Right on Point, left on Matrix, left on Angle, right on Geometry
    C. Left on Logic, right on Math, right on Point, right on Algebra, right on Angle, left on Geometry
    D. Left on Point, left on Matrix, left on Angle, right on Geometry

14. From Line to Logic. 14.____
    A. Left on Point, right on Algebra, right on Logic
    B. Right on Point, left on Math, left on Logic
    C. Left on Point, left on Algebra, right on Logic
    D. Right on Point, left on Matrix, right on Angle, left on Math, right on Logic

15. From Angle (between Math and Algebra) to Point. 15.____
    A. Left on Math, right on Point
    B. Left on Algebra, left on Point
    C. Left on Matrix, right on Point
    D. Left on Logic, right on Math, left on Point

16. From Matrix to Algebra. 16.____
    A. Right on Point, right on Math, left on Angle, left on Algebra
    B. Right on Angle, left on Algebra
    C. Right on Point, right on Algebra
    D. Left on Math, left on Point, right on Algebra

17. From Line to Geometry. 17.____
    A. Left on Point, right on Algebra, right on Angle, left on Geometry
    B. Right on Point, left on Math, left on Angle, right on Geometry
    C. Left on Point, left on Algebra, right on Logic, left on Angle, right on Geometry
    D. Right on Point, left on Matrix, left on Angle, right on Geometry

18. From Logic to Matrix. 18.____
    A. Right on Math, left on Point, left on Matrix
    B. Right on Math, right on Point, right on Matrix
    C. Left on Math, left on Angle, left on Matrix
    D. Right on Algebra, right on Angle, right on Matrix

Questions 19-25.

DIRECTIONS: For Questions 19 to 25, use the following map.

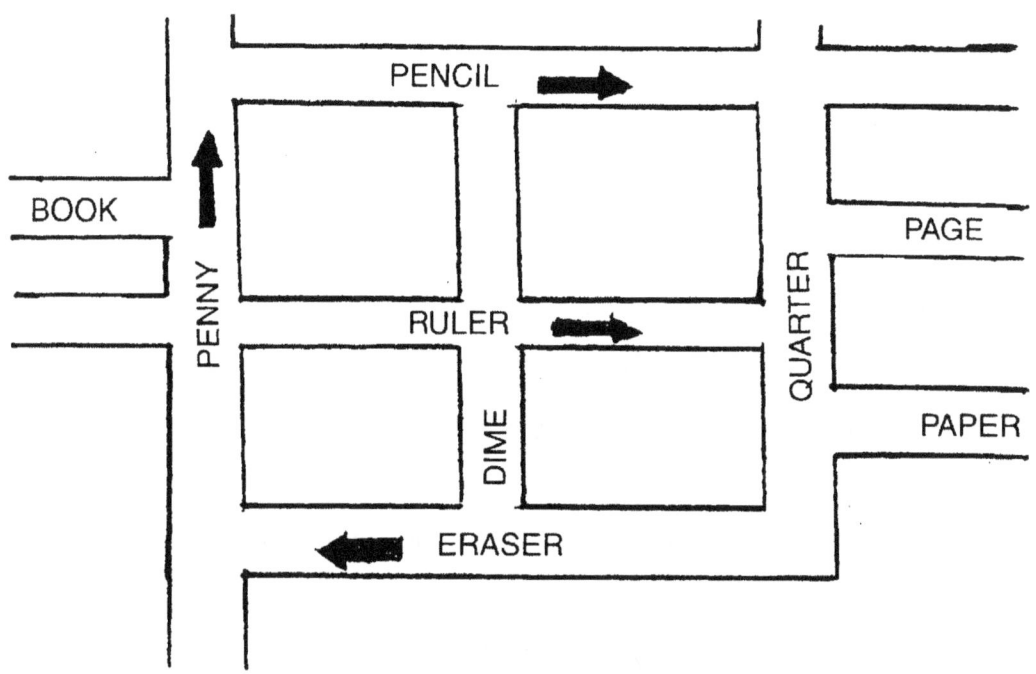

19. From Page to Dime.

    A. Right on Quarter, left on Pencil, left on Dime
    B. Left on Quarter, right on Ruler, right on Dime
    C. Right on Quarter, right on Pencil, left on Dime
    D. Left on Quarter, right on Eraser, right on Dime

19.____

20. From Penny to Eraser (between Dime and Quarter).

    A. Right on Pencil, right on Quarter, right on Eraser
    B. Right on Pencil, right on Dime, right on Eraser
    C. Right on Ruler, left on Quarter, right on Eraser
    D. Left on Ruler, right on Dime, right on Eraser

20.____

21. From Book to Quarter (south of Paper).

    A. Right on Penny, left on Ruler, right on Quarter
    B. Left on Penny, right on Ruler, right on Quarter
    C. Right on Penny, left on Eraser, left on Quarter
    D. Left on Penny, right on Pencil, right on Quarter

21.____

22. From Paper to Pencil (west of Dime).

    A. Right on Quarter, left on Pencil
    B. Left on Quarter, right on Eraser, right on Penny, right on Pencil
    C. Right on Quarter, right on Eraser, right on Dime, right on Pencil
    D. Left on Quarter, right on Eraser, right on Dime, left on Pencil

22.____

23. From Pencil (between Dime and Quarter) to Book.

    A. Right on Dime, right on Eraser, left on Penny, left on Book
    B. Right on Quarter, right on Ruler, right on Penny, left on Book
    C. Right on Quarter, right on Eraser, right on Penny, left on Book
    D. Right on Dime, right on Ruler, left on Book

24. From Penny (south of Eraser) to Dime (north of Ruler).

    A. Right on Ruler, left on Dime
    B. Right on Ruler, right on Dime
    C. Right on Pencil, left on Dime
    D. Right on Pencil, right on Quarter, right on Dime

25. From Ruler (west of Penny) to Paper.

    A. Right on Dime, left on Eraser, right on Paper
    B. Right on Quarter, left on Paper
    C. Left on Penny, right on Pencil, right on Quarter, right on Paper
    D. Right on Penny, left on Eraser, left on Quarter, right on Paper

KEY (CORRECT ANSWERS)

1. B
2. C
3. A
4. C
5. D

6. C
7. A
8. C
9. A
10. D

11. C
12. B
13. D
14. A
15. B

16. C
17. D
18. A
19. D
20. A

21. D
22. B
23. C
24. A
25. B

TEST 2

DIRECTIONS: Each map will be followed by several questions. For each question, you will be asked to go from one street to another street. There is ONLY ONE viable selection for each question, although it may not be the shortest route. Any street marked with either a ➡ or a ⬅ is a one-way street. Unmarked streets are two-ways.

In some cases, a PARTICULAR location on a street is mentioned in the question. This information should be used in arriving at a correct answer. All maps are hypothetical. *PRINT THE LETTER OF THE CORRECT ANSWER IN THE SPACE AT THE RIGHT.*

Questions 1-6.

DIRECTIONS: For Questions 1 to 6, use the following map.

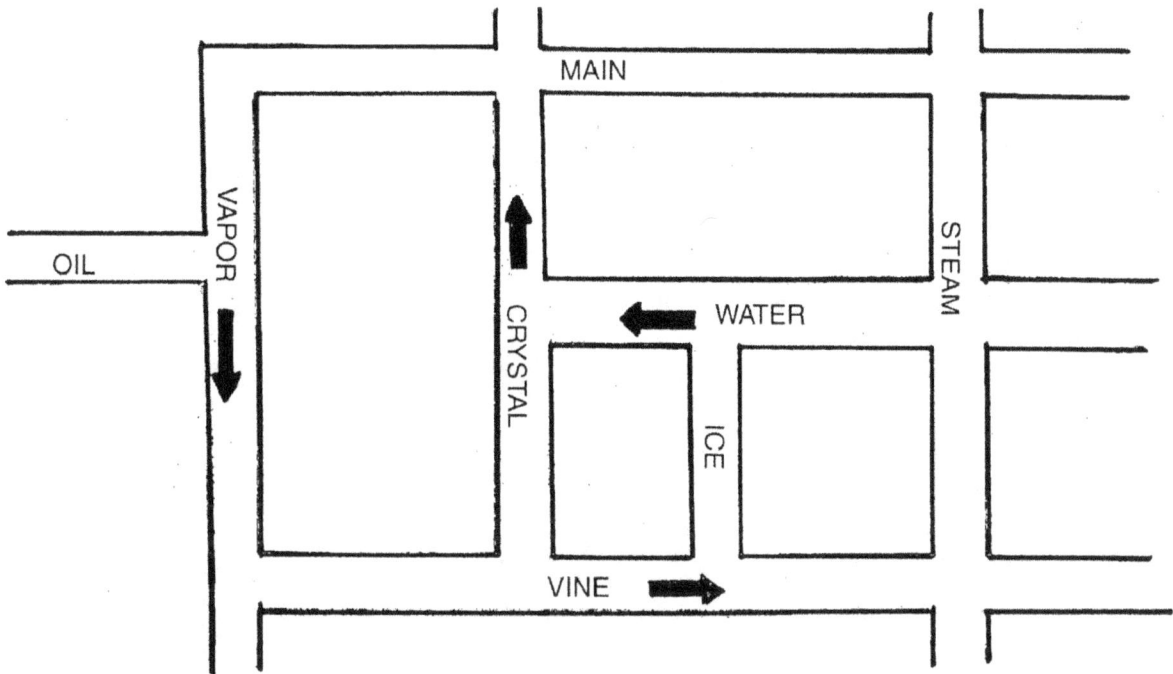

1. From Steam (north of Water) to Ice.

   A. Right on Water, left on Ice
   B. Right on Water, left on Crystal, left on Vine, left on Ice
   C. Left on Main, left on Crystal, right on Vine, right on Ice
   D. Left on Main, right on Vapor, left on Vine, right on Ice

2. From Oil to Main (east of Crystal).

   A. Right on Vapor, right on Crystal, left on Main
   B. Left on Vapor, right on Main
   C. Right on Vapor, left on Vine, left on Crystal, right on Main
   D. Left on Vapor, right on Vine, left on Main

1.____

2.____

41

3. From Water to Oil.   3.____

   A. Right on Crystal, left on Vapor, right on Oil
   B. Left on Crystal, right on Vine, right on Vapor, left on Oil
   C. Right on Crystal, left on Main, left on Vapor, right on Oil
   D. Left on Ice, right on Vapor, left on Oil

4. From Vine (between Crystal and Ice) to Crystal.   4.____

   A. Left on Ice, right on Steam, left on Crystal
   B. Left on Ice, left on Water, right on Crystal
   C. Left on Ice, right on Water, left on Crystal
   D. Left on Ice, left on Steam, right on Crystal

5. From Main (between Crystal and Steam) to Vine (east of Ice).   5.____

   A. Left on Crystal, left on Vine
   B. Right on Steam, right on Vine
   C. Right on Steam, right on Water, left on Ice, left on Vine
   D. Right on Steam, right on Water, right on Crystal, right on Vine

6. From Ice to Crystal (south of Water).   6.____

   A. Left on Water, left on Crystal
   B. Right on Water, left on Steam, left on Main, left on Crystal
   C. Right on Vine, right on Crystal
   D. Left on Water, right on Crystal, left on Main, left on Vapor, left on Vine, left oh Crystal

Questions 7-12.

DIRECTIONS: For Questions 7 to 12, use the following map.

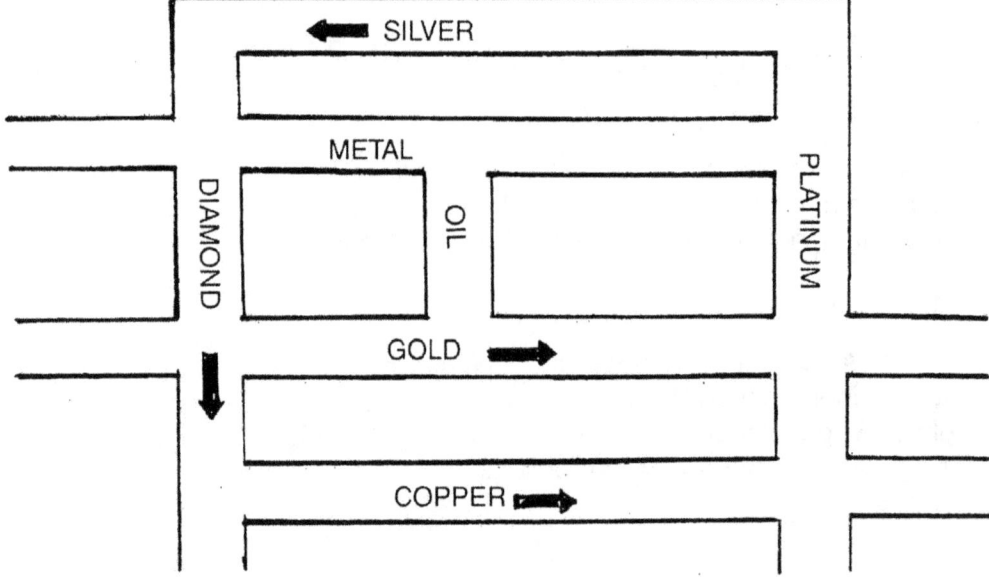

7. From Copper (west of Platinum) to Oil. 7.____

   A. Right on Diamond, right on Metal, right on Oil
   B. Left on Platinum, left on Gold, right on Oil
   C. Right on Diamond, right on Gold, left on Oil
   D. Left on Platinum, left on Metal, left on Oil

8. From Silver to Platinum (south of Copper). 8.____

   A. Left on Diamond, left on Gold, right on Platinum
   B. Left on Diamond, left on Copper, left on Platinum
   C. Right on Metal, left on Platinum
   D. Left on Diamond, left on Gold, left on Platinum

9. From Oil to Diamond (north of Metal). 9.____

   A. Left on Metal, left on Diamond
   B. Right on Gold, right on Diamond
   C. Left on Metal, right on Diamond
   D. Left on Gold, right on Copper, left on Diamond

10. From Platinum (between Gold and Copper) to Gold (between Oil and Diamond) 10.____

    A. Left on Metal, left on Oil, left on Gold
    B. Left on Silver, right on Diamond, right on Gold
    C. Left on Metal, left on Diamond, left on Gold
    D. Left on Silver, left on Oil, right on Gold

11. From Metal (west of Diamond) to Silver. 11.____

    A. Left on Diamond, right on Silver
    B. Left on Platinum, left on Silver
    C. Right on Platinum, right on Silver
    D. Right on Diamond, left on Silver

12. From Diamond (south of Copper) to Diamond (north of Metal). 12.____

    A. Right on Copper, left on Platinum, left on Silver, left on Diamond
    B. Right on Gold, left on Oil, left on Metal, left on Diamond
    C. Right on Copper, left on Platinum, left on Metal, right on Diamond
    D. Right on Copper, left on Platinum, left on Gold, right on Diamond

Questions 13-21.

DIRECTIONS: For Questions 13 to 21, use the following map.

4 (#2)

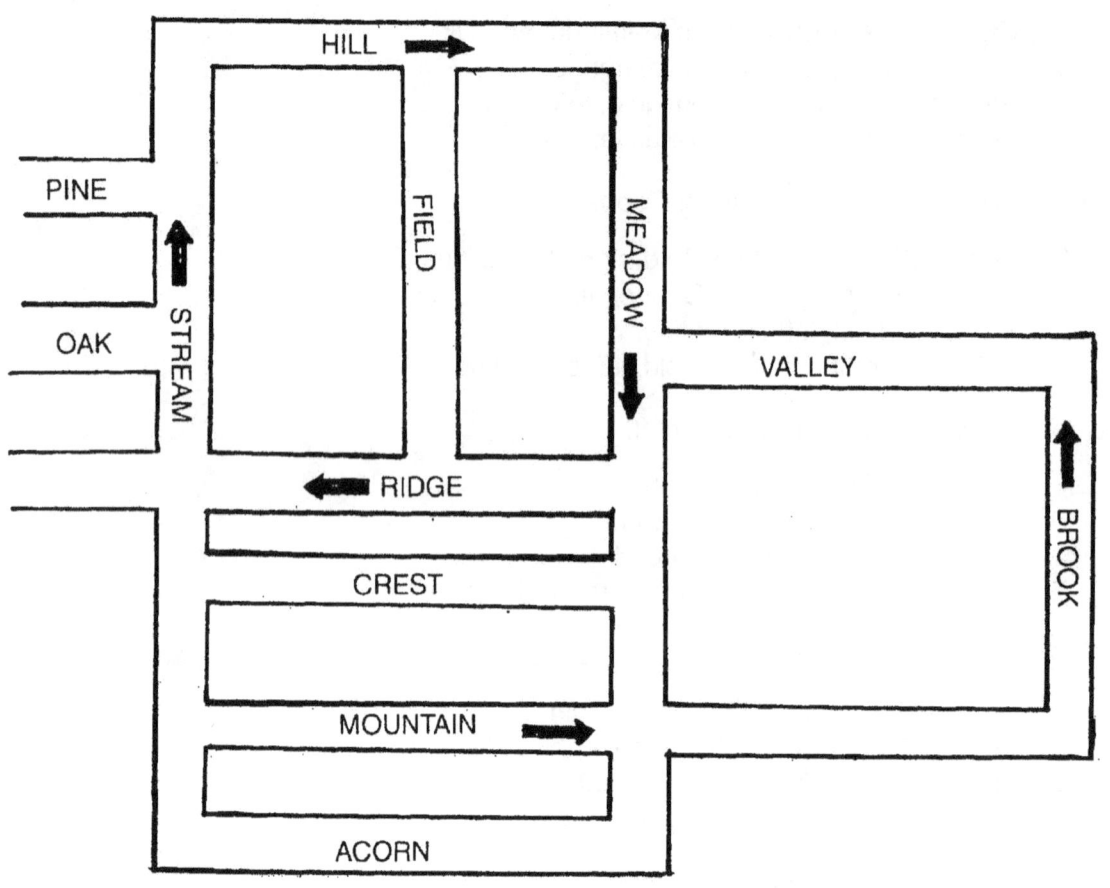

13. From Crest to Field.

   A. Left on Meadow, left on Ridge, right on Field
   B. Right on Stream, right on Hill, left on Field
   C. Right on Meadow, right on Ridge, left on Field
   D. Right on Stream, right on Hill, right on Field

14. From Valley to Oak.

   A. Left on Meadow, right on Mountain, left on Stream, left on Oak
   B. Left on Meadow, right on Ridge, right on Stream, left on Oak
   C. Right on Meadow, left on Hill, left on Stream, right on Oak
   D. Left on Meadow, left on Crest, right on Stream, left on Oak

15. From Field to Mountain (east of Meadow).

   A. Right on Hill, right on Meadow, left on Mountain
   B. Right on Ridge, right on Stream, left on Mountain
   C. Left on Ridge, right on Meadow, right on Mountain
   D. Right on Hill, left on Stream, right on Mountain

16. From Pine to Ridge (east of Field).

   A. Left on Stream, right on Hill, right on Field, right on Ridge
   B. Right on Stream, left on Ridge

5 (#2)

    C. Left on Stream, left on Field, left on Ridge
    D. Left on Stream, right on Hill, right on Meadow, right on Ridge

17. From Brook to Mountain (west of Meadow).   17.____

    A. Left on Valley, left on Meadow, right on Acorn, right on Stream, right on Mountain
    B. Left on Valley, left on Meadow, right on Mountain
    C. Left on Valley, right on Meadow, right on Ridge, left on Stream, left on Mountain
    D. Left on Meadow, right on Mountain

18. From Acorn to Meadow (between Crest and Ridge).   18.____

    A. Right on Stream, right on Mountain, left on Meadow
    B. Left on Stream, left on Crest, right on Meadow
    C. Right on Stream, right on Hill, right on Meadow
    D. Right on Stream, right on Crest, right on Meadow

19. From Ridge (east of Field) to Brook.   19.____

    A. Right on Meadow, left on Mountain, left on Brook
    B. Left on Stream, left on Crest, right on Meadow, left on Mountain, left on Brook
    C. Left on Meadow, right on Valley, right on Brook
    D. Right on Field, right on Hill, right on Meadow, left on Mountain, left on Brook

20. From Meadow (between Crest and Mountain) to Oak.   20.____

    A. Right on Acorn, right on Stream, left on Oak
    B. Right on Crest, right on Stream, left on Oak
    C. Right on Mountain, right on Stream, left on Oak
    D. Left on Hill, left on Stream, right on Oak

21. From Acorn to Ridge (west of Field).   21.____

    A. Left on Meadow, left on Ridge
    B. Right on Mountain, left on Brook, left on Valley, right on Meadow, left on Ridge
    C. Right on Stream, right on Hill, right on Field, right on Ridge
    D. Right on Stream, right on Mountain, left on Meadow, left on Ridge

Questions 22-25.

DIRECTIONS: For Questions 22 to 25, use the following map.

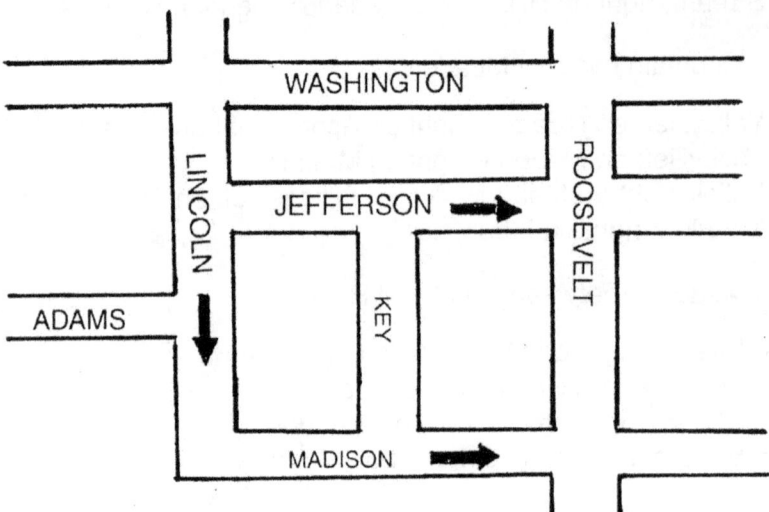

22. From Roosevelt (south of Madison) to Adams.

    A. Left on Washington, right on Lincoln, right on Adams
    B. Left on Jefferson, left on Lincoln, right on Adams
    C. Left on Washington, left on Lincoln, right on Adams
    D. Right on Jefferson, right on Key, right on Lincoln, left on Adams

23. From Madison (west of Key) to Jefferson (east of Roosevelt).

    A. Left on Roosevelt, left on Jefferson
    B. Left on Key, right on Jefferson
    C. Left on Key, left on Jefferson
    D. Left on Roosevelt, right on Washington, right on Jefferson

24. From Lincoln (south of Jefferson) to Adams.

    A. Right on Jefferson, right on Key, right on Madison, left on Adams
    B. Left on Jefferson, left on Lincoln, right on Adams
    C. Left on Washington, right on Lincoln, left on Adams
    D. Left on Madison, left on Roosevelt, left on Washington, left on Lincoln, right on Adams

25. From Washington (between Lincoln and Roosevelt) to Key.

    A. Right on Lincoln, left on Jefferson, right on Key
    B. Right on Roosevelt, right on Jefferson, left on Key
    C. Right on Roosevelt, right on Madison, right on Key
    D. Left on Lincoln, left on Madison, left on Key

KEY (CORRECT ANSWERS)

1. A
2. C
3. C
4. B
5. C

6. D
7. D
8. A
9. C
10. C

11. B
12. A
13. D
14. B
15. A

16. D
17. A
18. C
19. D
20. A

21. C
22. C
23. B
24. D
25. D

EXAMINATION SECTION
TEST 1

DIRECTIONS: Each question or incomplete statement is followed by several suggested answers or completions. Select the one that BEST answers the question or completes the statement. *PRINT THE LETTER OF THE CORRECT ANSWER IN THE SPACE AT THE RIGHT.*

1. In public agencies, communications should be based PRIMARILY on a
    A. two-way flow from the top down and from the bottom up, most of which should be given in writing to avoid ambiguity
    B. multi-direction flow among all levels and with outside persons
    C. rapid, internal one-way flow from the top down
    D. two-way flow of information, most of which should be given orally for purposes of clarity

2. In some organizations, changes in policy or procedures are often communicated by word of mouth from supervisors to employees with no prior discussion or exchange of viewpoints with employees.
    This procedure often produces employee dissatisfaction CHIEFLY because
    A. information is mostly unusable since a considerable amount of time is required to transmit information
    B. lower-level supervisors tend to be excessively concerned with minor details
    C. management has failed to seek employees' advice before making changes
    D. valuable staff time is lost between decision-making and the implementation of decisions

3. For good letter writing, you should try to visualize the person to whom you are writing, especially if you know him.
    Of the following rules, it is LEAST helpful in such visualization to think of
    A. the person's likes and dislikes, his concerns, and his needs
    B. what you would be likely to say if speaking in person
    C. what you would expect to be asked if speaking in person
    D. your official position in order to be certain that your words are proper

4. One approach to good informal letter writing is to make letters and conversational.
    All of the following practices will usually help to do this EXCEPT:
    A. If possible, use a style which is similar to the style used when speaking
    B. Substitute phrases for single words (e.g., *at the present time* for *now*)
    C. Use contractions of words (e.g., *you're* for *you are*)
    D. Use ordinary vocabulary when possible

5. All of the following rules will aid in producing clarity in report-writing EXCEPT:
   A. Give specific details or examples, if possible
   B. Keep related words close together in each sentence
   C. Present information in sequential order
   D. Put several thoughts or ideas in each paragraph

6. The one of the following statements about public relations which is MOST accurate is that
   A. in the long run, appearance gains better results than performance
   B. objectivity is decreased if outside public relations consultants are employed
   C. public relations is the responsibility of every employee
   D. public relations should be based on a formal publicity program

7. The form of communication which is usually considered to be MOST personally directed to the intended recipient is the
   A. brochure   B. film   C. letter   D. radio

8. In general, a document that presents an organization's views or opinions on a particular topic is MOST accurately known as a
   A. tear sheet   B. position paper
   C. flyer   D. journal

9. Assume that you have been asked to speak before an organization of persons who oppose a newly announced program in which you are involved. You feel tense about talking to this group.
   Which of the following rules generally would be MOST useful in gaining rapport when speaking before the audience?
   A. Impress them with your experience
   B. Stress all areas of disagreement
   C. Talk to the group as to one person
   D. Use formal grammar and language

10. An organization must have an effective public relations program since, at its best, public relations is a bridge to change.
    All of the following statements about communication and human behavior have validity EXCEPT:
    A. People are more likely to talk about controversial matters with like-minded people than with those holding other views
    B. The earlier an experience, the more powerful its effect since it influences how later experiences will be interpreted
    C. In periods of social tension, official sources gain increased believability
    D. Those who are already interested in a topic are the ones who are most open to receive new communications about it

11. An employee should be encouraged to talk easily and frankly when he is dealing with his supervisor.
    In order to encourage such free communication, it would be MOST appropriate for a supervisor to behave in a(n)
    A. sincere manner; assure the employee that you will deal with him honestly and openly
    B. official manner; you are a supervisor and must always act formally with subordinates
    C. investigative manner; you must probe and question to get to a basis of trust
    D. unemotional manner; the employee's emotions and background should play no part in your dealings with him

12. Research findings show that an increase in free communication within an agency GENERALLY results in which one of the following?
    A. Improved morale and productivity
    B. Increased promotional opportunities
    C. An increase in authority
    D. A spirit of honesty

13. Assume that you are a supervisor and your superiors have given you a new-type procedure to be followed.
    Before passing this information on to your subordinates, the one of the following actions that you should take FIRST is to
    A. ask your superiors to send out a memorandum to the entire staff
    B. clarify the procedure in your own mind
    C. set up a training course to provide instruction on the new procedure
    D. write a memorandum to your subordinates

14. Communication is necessary for an organization to be effective.
    The one of the following which is LEAST important for most communication systems is that
    A. messages are sent quickly and directly to the person who needs them to operate
    B. information should be conveyed understandably and accurately
    C. the method used to transmit information should be kept secret so that security can be maintained
    D. senders of messages must know how their messages are received and acted upon

15. Which one of the following is the CHIEF advantage of listening willingly to subordinates and encouraging them to talk freely and honestly?
    It
    A. reveals to supervisors the degree to which ideas that are passed down are accepted by subordinates
    B. reduces the participation of subordinates in the operation of the department
    C. encourages subordinates to try for promotion
    D. enables supervisors to learn more readily what the *grapevine* is saying

16. A supervisor may be informed through either oral or written reports.
    Which one of the following is an ADVANTAGE of using oral reports?
    A. There is no need for a formal record of the report.
    B. An exact duplicate of the report is not easily transmitted to others.
    C. A good oral report requires little time for preparation.
    D. An oral report involves two-way communication between a subordinate and his supervisor.

17. Of the following, the MOST important reason why supervisors should communicate effectively with the public is to
    A. improve the public's understanding of information that is important for them to know
    B. establish a friendly relationship
    C. obtain information about the kinds of people who come to the agency
    D. convince the public that services are adequate

18. Supervisors should generally NOT use phrases like *too hard*, *too easy*, and *a lot* PRINCIPALLY because such phrases
    A. may be offensive to some minority groups
    B. are too informal
    C. mean different things to different people
    D. are difficult to remember

19. The ability to communicate clearly and concisely is an important element in effective leadership.
    Which of the following statements about oral and written communication is GENERALLY true?
    A. Oral communication is more time-consuming.
    B. Written communication is more likely to be misinterpreted.
    C. Oral communication is useful only in emergencies.
    D. Written communication is useful mainly when giving information to fewer than twenty people.

20. Rumors can often have harmful and disruptive effects on an organization.
    Which one of the following is the BEST way to prevent rumors from becoming a problem?
    A. Refuse to act on rumors, thereby making them less believable.
    B. Increase the amount of information passed along by the *grapevine*.
    C. Distribute as much factual information as possible.
    D. Provide training in report writing.

21. Suppose that a subordinate asks you about a rumor he has heard. The rumor deals with a subject which your superiors consider *confidential*.
    Which of the following BEST describes how you should answer the subordinate? Tell

A. the subordinate that you don't make the rules and that he should speak to higher ranking officials
B. the subordinate that you will ask your superior for information
C. him only that you cannot comment on the matter
D. him the rumor is not true

22. Supervisors often find it difficult to *get their message across* when instructing newly appointed employees in their various duties.
The MAIN reason for this is generally that the
    A. duties of the employees have increased
    B. supervisor is often so expert in his area that he fails to see it from the learner's point of view
    C. supervisor adapts his instruction to the slowest learner in the group
    D. new employees are younger, less concerned with job security and more interested in fringe benefits

22._____

23. Assume that you are discussing a job problem with an employee under your supervision. During the discussion, you see that the man's eyes are turning away from you and that he is not paying attention.
In order to get the man's attention, you should FIRST
    A. ask him to look you in the eye
    B. talk to him about sports
    C. tell him he is being very rude
    D. change your tone of voice

23._____

24. As a supervisor, you may find it necessary to conduct meetings with your subordinates.
Of the following, which would be MOST helpful in assuring that a meeting accomplishes the purpose for which it was called?
    A. Give notice of the conclusions you would like to reach at the start of the meeting.
    B. Delay the start of the meeting until everyone is present.
    C. Write down points to be discussed in proper sequence.
    D. Make sure everyone is clear on whatever conclusions have been reached and on what must be done after the meeting.

24._____

25. Every supervisor will occasionally be called upon to deliver a reprimand to a subordinate. If done properly, this can greatly help an employee improve his performance.
Which one of the following is NOT a good practice to follow when giving a reprimand?
    A. Maintain your composure and temper
    B. Reprimand a subordinate in the presence of other employees so they can learn the same lesson
    C. Try to understand why the employee was not able to perform satisfactorily
    D. Let your knowledge of the man involved determine the exact nature of the reprimand

25._____

KEY (CORRECT ANSWERS)

1.	C	11.	A
2.	B	12.	A
3.	D	13.	B
4.	B	14.	C
5.	D	15.	A
6.	C	16.	D
7.	C	17.	A
8.	B	18.	C
9.	C	19.	B
10.	C	20.	C

21. B
22. B
23. D
24. D
25. B

TEST 2

DIRECTIONS: Each question or incomplete statement is followed by several suggested answers or completions. Select the one that BEST answers the question or completes the statement. *PRINT THE LETTER OF THE CORRECT ANSWER IN THE SPACE AT THE RIGHT.*

1. Usually one thinks of communication as a single step, essentially that of transmitting an idea.
   Actually, however, this is only part of a total process, the FIRST step of which should be
   A. the prompt dissemination of the idea to those who may be affected by it
   B. motivating those affected to take the required action
   C. clarifying the idea in one's own mind
   D. deciding to whom the idea is to be communicated

2. Research studies on patterns of informal communication have concluded that most individuals in a group tend to be passive recipients of news, while a few make it their business to spread it around in an organization.
   With this conclusion in mind, it would be MOST correct for the supervisor to attempt to identify these few individuals and
   A. give them the complete facts on important matters in advance of others
   B. inform the other subordinates of the identity of these few individuals so that their influence may be minimized
   C. keep them straight on the facts on important matters
   D. warn them to cease passing along any information to others

3. The one of the following which is the PRINCIPAL advantage of making an oral report is that it
   A. affords an immediate opportunity for two-way communication between the subordinate and superior
   B. is an easy method for the superior to use in transmitting information to others of equal rank
   C. saves the time of all concerned
   D. permits more precise pinpointing of praise or blame by means of follow-up questions by the superior

4. An agency may sometimes undertake a public relations program of a defensive nature.
   With reference to the use of defensive public relations, it would be MOST correct to state that it
   A. is bound to be ineffective since defensive statements, even though supported by factual data, can never hope to even partly overcome the effects of prior unfavorable attacks
   B. proves that the agency has failed to establish good relationships with newspapers, radio stations, or other means of publicity

C. shows that the upper echelons of the agency have failed to develop sound public relations procedures and techniques
D. is sometimes required to aid morale by protecting the agency from unjustified criticism and misunderstanding of policies or procedures

5. Of the following factors which contribute to possible undesirable public attitudes towards an agency, the one which is MOST susceptible to being changed by the efforts of the individual employee in an organization is that
   A. enforcement of unpopular regulations as offended many individuals
   B. the organization itself has an unsatisfactory reputation
   C. the public is not interested in agency matters
   D. there are many errors in judgment committed by individual subordinates

6. It is not enough for an agency's services to be of a high quality; attention must also be given to the acceptability of these services to the general public.
   This statement is GENERALLY
   A. *false*; a superior quality of service automatically wins public support
   B. *true*; the agency cannot generally progress beyond the understanding and support of the public
   C. *false*; the acceptance by the public of agency services determines their quality
   D. *true*; the agency is generally unable to engage in any effective enforcement activity without public support

7. Sustained agency participation in a program sponsored by a community organization is MOST justified when
   A. the achievement of agency objectives in some area depends partly on the activity of this organization
   B. the community organization is attempting to widen the base of participation in all community affairs
   C. the agency is uncertain as to what the community wants
   D. the agency is uncertain as to what the community wants

8. Of the following, the LEAST likely way in which a records system may serve a supervisor is in
   A. developing a sympathetic and cooperative public attitude toward the agency
   B. improving the quality of supervision by permitting a check on the accomplishment of subordinates
   C. permit a precise prediction of the exact incidences in specific categories for the following year
   D. helping to take the guesswork out of the distribution of the agency

9. Assuming that the *grapevine* in any organization is virtually indestructible, the one of the following which it is MOST important for management to understand is:
   A. What is being spread by means of the *grapevine* and the reason for spreading it
   B. What is being spread by means of the *grapevine* and how it is being spread
   C. Who is involved in spreading the information that is on the *grapevine*
   D. Why those who are involved in spreading the information are doing so

10. When the supervisor writes a report concerning an investigation to which he has been assigned, it should be LEAST intended to provide
    A. a permanent official record of relevant information gathered
    B. a summary of case findings limited to facts which tend to indicate the guilt of a suspect
    C. a statement of the facts on which higher authorities may base a corrective or disciplinary action
    D. other investigators with information so that they may continue with other phases of the investigation

11. In survey work, questionnaires rather than interviews are sometimes used. The one of the following which is a DISADVANTAGE of the questionnaire method as compared with the interview is the
    A. difficulty of accurately interpreting the results
    B. problem of maintaining anonymity of the participant
    C. fact that it is relatively uneconomical
    D. requirement of special training for the distribution of questionnaires

12. in his contacts with the public, an employee should attempt to create a good climate of support for his agency.
    This statement is GENERALLY
    A. *false*; such attempts are clearly beyond the scope of his responsibility
    B. *true*; employees of an agency who come in contact with the public have the opportunity to affect public relations
    C. *false*; such activity should be restricted to supervisors trained in public relations techniques
    D. *true*; the future expansion of the agency depends to a great extent on continued public support of the agency

13. The repeated use by a supervisor of a call for volunteers to get a job done is objectionable MAINLY because it
    A. may create a feeling of animosity between the volunteers and the non-volunteers
    B. may indicate that the supervisor is avoiding responsibility for making assignments which will be most productive
    C. is an indication that the supervisor is not familiar with the individual capabilities of his men
    D. is unfair to men who, for valid reasons, do not, or cannot volunteer

14. Of the following statements concerning subordinates' expressions to a supervisor of their opinions and feelings concerning work situations, the one which is MOST correct is that
    A. by listening and responding to such expressions the supervisor encourages the development of complaints
    B. the lack of such expressions should indicate to the supervisor that there is a high level of job satisfaction
    C. the more the supervisor listens to and responds to such expressions, the more he demonstrates lack of supervisory ability
    D. by listening and responding to such expressions, the supervisor will enable many subordinates to understand and solve their own problems on the job

14.____

15. In attempting to motivate employees, rewards are considered preferable to punishment PRIMARILY because
    A. punishment seldom has any effect on human behavior
    B. punishment usually results in decreased production
    C. supervisors find it difficult to punish
    D. rewards are more likely to result in willing cooperation

15.____

16. In an attempt to combat the low morale in his organization, a high level supervisor publicized an *open-door policy* to allow employees who wished to do so to come to him with their complaints.
Which of the following is LEAST likely to account for the fact that no employee came in with a complaint?
    A. Employees are generally reluctant to go over the heads of their immediate supervisor.
    B. The employees did not feel that management would help them.
    C. The low morale was not due to complaints associated with the job.
    D. The employees felt that they had more to lose than to gain.

16.____

17. It is MOST desirable to use written instructions rather than oral instructions for a particular job when
    A. a mistake on the job will not be serious
    B. the job can be completed in a short time
    C. there is no need to explain the job minutely
    D. the job involves many details

17.____

18. If you receive a telephone call regarding a matter which your office does not handle, you should FIRST
    A. give the caller the telephone number of the proper office so that he can dial again
    B. offer to transfer the caller to the proper office
    C. suggest that the caller re-dial since he probably dialed incorrectly
    D. tell the caller he has reached the wrong office and then hang up

18.____

19. When you answer the telephone, the MOST important reason for identifying yourself and your organization is to
    A. give the caller time to collect his or her thoughts
    B. impress the caller with your courtesy
    C. inform the caller that he or she has reached the right number
    D. set a business-like tone at the beginning of the conversation

19.____

20. As soon as you pick up the phone, a very angry caller begins immediately to complain about city agencies and *red tape*. He says that he has been shifted to two or three different offices. It turs out that he is seeking information which is not immediately available to you. You believe, you know, however, where it can be found.
    Which of the following actions is the BEST one for you to take?
    A. To eliminate all confusion, suggest that the caller write the agency stating explicitly what he wants.
    B. Apologize by telling the caller how busy city agencies now are, but also tell him directly that you do not have the information he needs.
    C. Ask for the caller's telephone number and assure him you will call back after you have checked further.
    D. Give the caller the name and telephone number of the person who might be able to help, but explain that you are not positive he will get results/

20.____

21. Which of the following approaches usually provides the BEST communication in the objectives and values of a new program which is to be introduced?
    A. A general written description of the program by the program manager for review by those who share responsibility
    B. An effective verbal presentation by the program manager to those affected
    C. Development of the plan and operational approach in carrying out the program by the program manager assisted by his key subordinates
    D. Development of the plan by the program manager's supervisor

21.____

22. What is the BEST approach for introducing change?
    A
    A. combination of written and also verbal communication to all personnel affected by the change
    B. general bulletin to all personnel
    C. meeting pointing out all the values of the new approach
    D. written directive to key personnel

22.____

23. Of the following, committees are BEST used for
    A. advising the head of the organization
    B. improving functional work
    C. making executive decisions
    D. making specific planning decisions

23.____

24. An effective discussion leader is one who
    A. announces the problem and his preconceived solution at the start of the discussion
    B. guides and directs the discussion according to pre-arranged outline
    C. interrupts or corrects confused participants to save time
    D. permits anyone to say anything at any time

25. The human relations movement in management theory is basically concerned with
    A. counteracting employee unrest
    B. eliminating the *time and motion* man
    C. interrelationships among individuals in organizations
    D. the psychology of the worker

KEY (CORRECT ANSWERS)

1.	C	11.	A
2.	C	12.	B
3.	A	13.	B
4.	D	14.	D
5.	D	15.	D
6.	B	16.	C
7.	A	17.	D
8.	C	18.	B
9.	A	19.	C
10.	B	20.	C

21.	C
22.	A
23.	A
24.	B
25.	C

READING COMPREHENSION
UNDERSTANDING AND INTERPRETING WRITTEN MATERIAL
EXAMINATION SECTION
TEST 1

DIRECTIONS: Each question or incomplete statement is followed by several suggested answers or completions. Select the one that BEST answers the question or completes the statement. *PRINT THE LETTER OF THE CORRECT ANSWER IN THE SPACE AT THE RIGHT.*

Questions 1-4.

DIRECTIONS: Questions 1 through 4 are to be answered SOLELY on the basis of the following passage.

Those engaged in the exercise of First Amendment rights by pickets, marches, parades, and open-air assemblies are not exempted from obeying valid local traffic ordinances. In a recent pronouncement, Mr. Justice Baxter, speaking for the Supreme Court, wrote:

The rights of free speech and assembly, while fundamental to our democratic society, still do not mean that everyone with opinions or beliefs to express may address a group at any public place and at any time. The constitutional guarantee of liberty implies the existence of an organized society maintaining public order, without which liberty itself would be lost in the excesses of anarchy. The control of travel on the streets is a clear example of governmental responsibility to insure this necessary order. A restriction in that relation, designed to promote the public convenience in the interest of all, and not susceptible to abuses of discriminatory application, cannot be disregarded by the attempted exercise of some civil rights which, in other circumstances, would be entitled to protection. One would not be justified in ignoring the familiar red light because this was thought to be a means of social protest. Governmental authorities have the duty and responsibility to keep their streets open and available for movement. A group of demonstrators could not insist upon the right to cordon off a street, or entrance to a public or private building, and allow no one to pass who did not agree to listen to their exhortations.

1. Which of the following statements BEST reflects Mr. Justice Baxter's view of the relationship between liberty and public order?

    A. Public order cannot exist without liberty.
    B. Liberty cannot exist without public order.
    C. The existence of liberty undermines the existence of public order.
    D. The maintenance of public order insures the existence of liberty.

1.____

2. According to the above passage, local traffic ordinances result from

    A. governmental limitations on individual liberty
    B. governmental responsibility to insure public order
    C. majority rule as determined by democratic procedures
    D. restrictions on expression of dissent

2.____

3. The above passage suggests that government would be acting improperly if a local traffic ordinance

    A. was enforced in a discriminatory manner
    B. resulted in public inconvenience
    C. violated the right of free speech and assembly
    D. was not essential to public order

4. Of the following, the MOST appropriate title for the above passage is

    A. THE RIGHTS OF FREE SPEECH AND ASSEMBLY
    B. ENFORCEMENT OF LOCAL TRAFFIC ORDINANCES
    C. FIRST AMENDMENT RIGHTS AND LOCAL TRAFFIC ORDINANCES
    D. LIBERTY AND ANARCHY

Questions 5-8

DIRECTIONS: Questions 5 through 8 are to be answered SOLELY on the basis of the following passage

On November 8, 1976, the Supreme Court refused to block the payment of Medicaid funds for elective abortions. The Court's action means that a new Federal statute that bars the use of Federal funds for abortions unless abortion is necessary to save the life of the mother will not go into effect for many months, if at all.

A Federal District Court in Brooklyn ruled the following month that the statute was unconstitutional and ordered that Federal reimbursement for the costs of abortions continue on the same basis as reimbursements for the costs of pregnancy and childbirth-related services.

Technically, what the Court did today was to deny a request by Senator Howard Ramsdell and others for a stay blocking enforcement of the District Court order pending appeal. The Court's action was a victory for New York City. The City's Health and Hospitals Corporation initiated one of the two lawsuits challenging the new statute that led to the District Court's decision. The Corporation also opposed the request for a Supreme Court stay of that decision, telling the Court in a memorandum that a stay would subject the Corporation to a *grave and irreparable injury.*

5. According to the above passage, it would be CORRECT to state that the Health and Hospitals Corporation

    A. joined Senator Ramsdell in his request for a stay
    B. opposed the statute which limited reimbursement for the cost of abortions
    C. claimed that it would experience a loss if the District Court order was enforced
    D. appealed the District Court decision

6. The above passage indicates that the Supreme Court acted in DIRECT response to

    A. a lawsuit initiated by the Health and Hospitals Corporation
    B. a ruling by a Federal District Court
    C. a request for a stay
    D. the passage of a new Federal statute

7. According to the above passage, it would be CORRECT to state that the Supreme Court

   A. blocked enforcement of the District Court order
   B. refused a request for a stay to block enforcement of the Federal statute
   C. ruled that the new Federal statute was unconstitutional
   D. permitted payment of Federal funds for abortion to continue

8. Following are three statements concerning abortion that might be correct:
   I. Abortion costs are no longer to be Federally reimbursed on the same basis as those for pregnancy and childbirth
   II. Federal funds have not been available for abortions except to save the life of the mother
   III. Medicaid has paid for elective abortions in the past

   According to the passage above, which of the following CORRECTLY classifies the above statements into those that are true and those that are not true?

   A. I is true, but II and III are not.
   B. I and III are true, but II is not.
   C. I and II are true, but III is not.
   D. III is true, but I and II are not.

Questions 9-12.

DIRECTIONS: Questions 9 through 12 are to be answered SOLELY on the basis of the following passage.

A person may use physical force upon another person when and to the extent he reasonably believes such to be necessary to defend himself or a third person from what he reasonably believes to be the use or imminent use of unlawful physical force by such other person, unless (a) the latter's conduct was provoked by the actor himself with intent to cause physical injury to another person; or (b) the actor was the initial aggressor; or (c) the physical force involved is the product of a combat by agreement not specifically authorized by law.

A person may not use deadly physical force upon another person under the circumstances specified above unless (a) he reasonably believes that such other person is using or is about to use deadly physical force. Even in such case, however, the actor may not use deadly physical force if he knows he can, with complete safety, as to himself and others avoid the necessity of doing so by retreating; except that he is under no duty to retreat if he is in his dwelling and is not the initial aggressor; or (b) he reasonably believes that such other person is committing or attempting to commit a kidnapping, forcible rape, or forcible sodomy.

9. Jones and Smith, who have not met before, get into an argument in a tavern. Smith takes a punch at Jones, but misses. Jones then hits Smith on the chin with his fist. Smith falls to the floor and suffers minor injuries.
   According to the above passage, it would be CORRECT to state that _____ justified in using physical force.

   A. only Smith was
   B. only Jones was
   C. both Smith and Jones were
   D. neither Smith nor Jones was

10. While walking down the street, Brady observes Miller striking Mrs. Adams on the head with his fist in an attempt to steal her purse.
According to the above passage, it would be CORRECT to state that Brady would

   A. not be justified in using deadly physical force against Miller since Brady can safely retreat
   B. be justified in using physical force against Miller but not deadly physical force
   C. not be justified in using physical force against Miller since Brady himself is not being attacked
   D. be justified in using deadly physical force

11. Winters is attacked from behind by Sharp, who attempts to beat up Winters with a blackjack. Winters disarms Sharp and succeeds in subduing him with a series of blows to the head. Sharp stops fighting and explains that he thought Winters was the person who had robbed his apartment a few minutes before, but now realizes his mistake.
According to the above passage, it would be CORRECT to state that

   A. Winters was justified in using physical force on Sharp only to the extent necessary to defend himself
   B. Winters was not justified in using physical force on Sharp since Sharp's attack was provoked by what he believed to be Winters' behavior
   C. Sharp was justified in using physical force on Winters since he reasonably believed that Winters had unlawfully robbed him
   D. Winters was justified in using physical force on Sharp only because Sharp was acting mistakenly in attacking him

12. Roberts hears a noise in the cellar of his home, and, upon investigation, discovers an intruder, Welch. Welch moves towards Roberts in a threatening manner, thrusts his hand into a bulging pocket, and withdraws what appears to be a gun. Roberts thereupon strikes Welch over the head with a golf club. He then sees that the *gun* is a toy. Welch later dies of head injuries. According to the above passage, it would be CORRECT to state that Roberts was

   A. justified in using deadly physical force because he reasonably believed Welch was about to use deadly physical force
   B. not justified in using deadly physical force
   C. justified in using deadly physical force only because he did not provoke Welch's conduct
   D. justified in using deadly physical force only because he was not the initial aggressor

Questions 13-16.

DIRECTIONS: Questions 13 through 16 are to be answered SOLELY on the basis of the following passage.

From the beginning, the Supreme Court has supervised the fairness of trials conducted by the Federal government. But the Constitution, as originally drafted, gave the court no such general authority in state cases. The court's power to deal with state cases comes from the Fourteenth Amendment, which became part of the Constitution in 1868. The crucial provision forbids any state to *deprive any person of life, liberty, or property without due process of law.*

The guarantee of *due process* would seem, at the least, to require fair procedure in criminal trials. But curiously the Supreme Court did not speak on the question for many decades. During that time, however, the due process clause was interpreted to bar *unreasonable* state economic regulations, such as minimum wage laws.

In 1915, there came the case of Leo M. Frank, a Georgian convicted of murder in a trial that he contended was dominated by mob hysteria. Historians now agree that there was such hysteria, with overtones of anti-semitism.

The Supreme Court held that it could not look past the findings of the Georgia courts that there had been no mob atmosphere at the trial. Justices Oliver Wendell Holmes and Charles Evans Hughes dissented, arguing that the constitutional guarantee would be *a barren one* if the Federal courts could not make their own inferences from the facts.

In 1923, the case of Moore v. Dempsey involved five Arkansas Blacks convicted of murder and sentenced to death in a community so aroused against them that at one point they were saved from lynching only by Federal troops. Witnesses against them were said to have been beaten into testifying.

The court, though not actually setting aside the convictions, directed a lower Federal court to hold a habeas corpus hearing to find out whether the trial had been fair, or whether the whole proceeding had been *a mask—that counsel, jury, and judge were swept to the fatal end by an irresistible wave of public passion.*

13. According to the above passage, the Supreme Court's INITIAL interpretation of the Fourteenth Amendment

    A. protected state supremacy in economic matters
    B. increased the scope of Federal jurisdiction
    C. required fair procedures in criminal trials
    D. prohibited the enactment of minimum wage laws

14. According to the above passage, the Supreme Court in the Frank case

    A. denied that there had been mob hysteria at the trial
    B. decided that the guilty verdict was supported by the evidence
    C. declined to question the state court's determination of the facts
    D. found that Leo Frank had not received *due process*

15. According to the above passage, the dissenting judges in the Frank case maintained that

    A. due process was an empty promise in the circumstances of that case
    B. the Federal courts could not guarantee certain provisions of the Constitution
    C. the Federal courts should not make their own inferences from the facts in state cases
    D. the Supreme Court had rendered the Constitution *barren*

16. Of the following, the MOST appropriate title for the above passage is 16.____
    A. THE CONDUCT OF FEDERAL TRIALS
    B. THE DEVELOPMENT OF STATES' RIGHTS: 1868-1923
    C. MOORE V. DEMPSEY: A CASE STUDY IN CRIMINAL JUSTICE
    D. DUE PROCESS-THE EVOLUTION OF A CONSTITUTIONAL CORNERSTONE

Questions 17-20.

DIRECTIONS: Questions 17 through 20 are to be answered SOLELY on the basis of the following passage.

The difficulty experienced in determining which party has the burden of proving payment or non-payment is due largely to a lack of consistency between the rules of pleading and the rules of proof. In some cases, a plaintiff is obligated by a rule of pleading to allege non-payment on his complaint, yet is not obligated to prove non-payment on the trial. An action upon a contract for the payment of money will serve as an illustration. In such a case, the plaintiff must allege non-payment in his complaint, but the burden of proving payment on the trial is upon the defendant. An important and frequently cited case on this problem is Conkling v. Weatherwax. In that case, the action was brought to establish and enforce a legacy as a lien upon real property. The defendant alleged in her answer that the legacy had been paid. There was no witness competent to testify for the plaintiff to show that the legacy had not been paid. Therefore, the question of the burden of proof became of primary importance since, if the plaintiff had the burden of proving non-payment, she must fail in her action; whereas if the burden of proof was on the defendant to prove payment, the plaintiff might win. The Court of Appeals held that the burden of proof was on the plaintiff. In the course of his opinion, Judge Vann attempted to harmonize the conflicting cases on this subject, and for that purpose formulated three rules. These rules have been construed and applied to numerous subsequent cases. As so construed and applied, these may be summarized as follows:

Rule 1. In an action upon a contract for the payment of money only, where the complaint does not allege a balance due over and above all payments made, the plaintiff must allege nonpayment in his complaint, but the burden of proving payment is upon the defendant. In such a case, payment is an affirmative defense which the defendant must plead in his answer. If the defendant fails to plead payment, but pleads a general denial instead, he will not be permitted to introduce evidence of payment.

Rule 2. Where the complaint sets forth a balance in excess of all payments, owing to the structure of the pleading, burden is upon the plaintiff to prove his allegation. In this case, the defendant is not required to plead payment as a defense in his answer but may introduce evidence of payment under a general denial.

Rule 3. When the action is not upon contract for the payment of money, but is upon an obligation created by operation of law, or is for the enforcement of a lien where non-payment of the amount secured is part of the cause of action, it is necessary both to allege and prove the fact of nonpayment.

17. In the above passage, the case of Conkling v. Weatherwax was cited PRIMARILY to illustrate 17.____

    A. a case where the burden of proof was on the defendant to prove payment
    B. how the question of the burden of proof can affect the outcome of a case
    C. the effect of a legacy as a lien upon real property
    D. how conflicting cases concerning the burden of proof were harmonized

18. According to the above passage, the pleading of payment is a defense in Rule(s) 18.____

    A. 1, but not Rules 2 and 3
    B. 2, but not Rules 1 and 3
    C. 1 and 3, but not Rule 2
    D. 2 and 3, but not Rule 1

19. The facts in Conkling v. Weatherwax CLOSELY resemble the conditions described in 19.____

    A. Rule #1
    B. Rule #2
    C. Rule #3
    D. none of the rules

20. The MAJOR topic of the above passage may BEST be described as 20.____

    A. determining the ownership of property
    B. providing a legal definition
    C. placing the burden of proof
    D. formulating rules for deciding cases

Questions 21-25.

DIRECTIONS: Questions 21 through 25 are to be answered SOLELY on the basis of the following passage.

The law is quite clear that evidence obtained in violation of Section 605 of the Federal Communications Act is not admissible in Federal court. However, the law as to the admissibility of evidence in state court is far from clear. Had the Supreme Court of the United States made the wiretap exclusionary rule applicable to the states, such confusion would not exist.

In the case of Alton v. Texas, the Supreme Court was called upon to determine whether wiretapping by state and local officers came within the proscription of the Federal statute and, if so, whether Section 605 required the same remedies for its vindication in state courts. In answer to the first question, Mr. Justice Minton, speaking for the court, flatly stated that Section 605 made it a federal crime for anyone to intercept telephone messages and divulge what he learned. The court went on to say that a state officer who testified in state court concerning the existence, contents, substance, purport, effect, or meaning of an intercepted conversation violated the Federal law and committed a criminal act. In regard to the second question, how-ever, the Supreme Court felt constrained by due regard for federal-state relations to answer in the negative. Mr. Justice Minton stated that the court would not presume, in the absence of a clear manifestation of congressional intent, that Congress intended to supersede state rules of evidence.

Because the Supreme Court refused to apply the exclusionary rule to wiretap evidence that was being used in state courts, the states respectively made this decision for themselves. According to hearings held before a congressional committee in 1975, six states authorize wiretapping by statute, 33 states impose total bans on wiretapping, and 11 states have no definite statute on the subject. For examples of extremes, a statute in Pennsylvania will be compared with a statute in New York.

The Pennsylvania statute provides that no communications by telephone or telegraph can be intercepted without permission of both parties. It also specifically prohibits such interception by public officials and provides that evidence obtained cannot be used in court.

The lawmakers in New York, recognizing the need for legal wire-tapping, authorized wiretapping by statute. A New York law authorizes the issuance of an ex parte order upon oath or affirmation for limited wiretapping. The aim of the New York law is to allow court-ordered wiretapping and to encourage the testimony of state officers concerning such wiretapping in court. The New York law was found to be constitutional by the New York State Supreme Court in 1975. Other states, including Oregon, Maryland, Nevada, and Massachusetts, enacted similar laws which authorize court-ordered wiretapping.

To add to this legal disarray, the vast majority of the states, including New Jersey and New York, permit wiretapping evidence to be received in court even though obtained in violation of the state laws and of Section 605 of the Federal act. However, some states, such as Rhode Island, have enacted statutory exclusionary rules which provide that illegally procured wiretap evidence is incompetent in civil as well as criminal actions.

21. According to the above passage, a state officer who testifies in New York State court concerning the contents of a conversation he overheard through a court-ordered wire-tap is in violation of _____ law.

    A. state law but not federal
    B. federal law but not state
    C. federal law and state
    D. neither federal nor state

22. According to the above passage, which of the following statements concerning states statutes on wiretapping is CORRECT?

    A. The number of states that impose total bans on wiretapping is three times as great as the number of states with no definite statute on wiretapping.
    B. The number of states having no definite statute on wiretapping is more than twice the number of states authorizing wiretapping.
    C. The number of states which authorize wiretapping by statute and the number of states having no definite statute on wiretapping exceed the number of states imposing total bans on wiretapping.
    D. More states authorize wiretapping by statute than impose total bans on wiretapping.

23. Following are three statements concerning wiretapping that might be valid:

    I. In Pennsylvania, only public officials may legally intercept telephone communications.
    II. In Rhode Island, evidence obtained through an illegal wiretap is incompetent in criminal, but not civil, actions.
    III. Neither Massachusetts nor Pennsylvania authorizes wiretapping by public officials.

    According to the above passage, which of the following CORRECTLY classifies these statements into those that are valid and those that are not?

    A. I is valid, but II and III are not.
    B. II is valid, but I and III are not.
    C. II and III are valid, but I is not.
    D. None of the statements is valid.

24. According to the above passage, evidence obtained in violation of Section 605 of the Federal Communications Act is inadmissible in

    A. federal court but not in any state courts
    B. federal court and all state courts
    C. all state courts but not in federal court
    D. federal court and some state courts

25. In regard to state rules of evidence, Mr. Justice Minton expressed the Court's opinion that Congress

    A. intended to supersede state rules of evidence, as manifested by Section 605 of the Federal Communications Act
    B. assumed that federal statutes would govern state rules of evidence in all wiretap cases
    C. left unclear whether it intended to supersede state rules of evidence
    D. precluded itself from superseding state rules of evidence through its regard for federal-state relations

KEY (CORRECT ANSWERS)

1. B
2. B
3. A
4. C
5. B

6. C
7. D
8. D
9. B
10. B

11. A
12. A
13. D
14. C
15. A

16. D
17. B
18. A
19. C
20. C

21. B
22. A
23. D
24. D
25. C

TEST 2

DIRECTIONS: Each question or incomplete statement is followed by several suggested answers or completions. Select the one that BEST answers the question or completes the Statement. *PRINT THE LETTER OF THE CORRECT ANSWER IN THE SPACE AT THE RIGHT.*

Questions 1-3.

DIRECTIONS: Questions 1 through 3 are to be answered SOLELY on the basis of the following passage.

The State Assembly has passed a bill that would require all state agencies, public authorities, and local governments to refuse bids in excess of $2,000 from any foreign firm or corporation. The only exceptions to this outright prohibition against public buying of foreign goods or services would be for products not available in this country, goods of a quality unobtainable from an American supplier, and products using foreign materials that are *substantially* manufactured in the United States.

This bill is a flagrant violation of the United States' officially espoused trade principles. It would add to the costs of state and local governments. It could provoke retaliatory action from many foreign governments against the state and other American producers, and foreign governments would be fully entitled to take such retaliatory action under the General Agreement on Tariffs and Trade, which the United States has signed.

The State Senate, which now has the Assembly bill before it, should reject this protectionist legislation out of enlightened regard for the interests of the taxpayers and producers of the State—as well as for those of the nation and its trading partners generally. In this time of unemployment and international monetary disorder, the State—with its reputation for intelligent and progressive law-making—should avoid contributing to what could become a tidal wave of protectionism here and overseas.

1. Under the requirements of the bill passed by the State Assembly, a bid from a foreign manufacturer in excess of $2,000 can be accepted by a state agency or local government only if it meets which one of the following requirements?
The

   A. bid is approved individually by the State Legislature
   B. bidder is willing to accept payment in United States currency
   C. bid is for an item of a quality unobtainable from an American supplier
   D. bid is for an item which would be more expensive if it were purchased from an American supplier

2. The author of the above passage feels that the bill passed by the State Assembly should be

   A. passed by the State Senate and put into effect
   B. passed by the State Senate but vetoed by the Governor
   C. reintroduced into the State Assembly and rejected
   D. rejected by the State Senate

3. The author of the above passage calls the practice of prohibiting purchase of products manufactured by foreign countries

   A. prohibition
   B. protectionism
   C. retaliatory action
   D. isolationism

Questions 4-7.

DIRECTIONS: Questions 4 through 7 are to be answered SOLELY on the basis of the following passage.

Data processing is by no means a new invention. In one form or another, it has been carried on throughout the entire history of civilization. In its most general sense, data processing means organizing data so that it can be used for a specific purpose-a procedure commonly known simply as *record-keeping* or *paperwork*. With the development of modern office equipment, and particularly with the recent introduction of computers, the techniques of data processing have become highly elaborate and sophisticated, but the basic purpose remains the same: Turning raw data into useful information.

The key concept here is usefulness. The data, or input, that is to be processed can be compared to the raw material that is to go into a manufacturing process. The information, or output, that results from data processing—like the finished product of a manufacturer—should be clearly usable. A collection of data has little value unless it is converted into information that serves a specific function.

4. The expression *paperwork*, as it is used in this passage,

   A. shows that the author regards such operations as a waste of time
   B. has the same general meaning as *data processing*
   C. refers to methods of record-keeping that are no longer in use
   D. indicates that the public does not understand the purpose of data processing

5. The above passage indicates that the use of computers has

   A. greatly simplified the clerical work in an office
   B. led to more complicated systems for the handling of data
   C. had no effect whatsoever on data processing
   D. made other modern office machines obsolete

6. Which of the following BEST expresses the basic principle of data processing as it is described in the above passage?

   A. Input-processing-output
   B. Historical record-keeping-modern techniques -specific functions
   C. Office equipment-computer-accurate data
   D. Raw material-manufacturer-retailer

7. According to the above passage, data processing may be described as

   A. a new management technique
   B. computer technology
   C. information output
   D. record-keeping

Questions 8-10.

DIRECTIONS: Questions 8 through 10 are to be answered SOLELY on the basis of the following passage.

A loan receipt is an instrument devised to permit the insurance company to bring an action against the wrongdoer in the name of the insured despite the fact that the insured no longer has any financial interest in the outcome. It provides, in effect, that the amount of the loss is advanced to the insured as a loan which is repayable only up to the extent of any recovery made from the wrongdoer. The insured further agrees to enter and prosecute suit against the wrongdoer in his own name. Such a receipt substitutes a loan for a payment for the purpose of permitting the insurance company to press its action against the wrongdoer in the name of the insured.

8. According to the above passage, the purpose behind the use of a loan receipt is to   8.____

    A. guarantee that the insurance company gets repayment from the person insured
    B. insure repayment of all expenditures to the named insured
    C. make it possible for the insurance company to sue in the name of the policyowner
    D. prevent the wrongdoer from escaping the natural consequences of his act

9. According to the above passage, the amount of the loan which must be paid back to the insurance company equals but does NOT exceed the amount   9.____

    A. of the loss
    B. on the face of the policy
    C. paid to the insured
    D. recovered from the wrongdoer

10. According to the above passage, by giving a loan receipt, the person insured agrees to   10.____

    A. a suit against the wrongdoer in his own name
    B. forego any financial gain from the outcome of the suit
    C. institute an action on behalf of the insurance company
    D. repay the insurance company for the loan received

Questions 11-12.

DIRECTIONS: Questions 11 and 12 are to be answered SOLELY on the basis of the following passage.

Open air markets originally came into existence spontaneously when groups of pushcart peddlers congregated in spots where business was good. Good business induced them to return to these spots daily and, thus, unofficial open air markets arose. These peddlers paid no fees, and the city received no revenue from them. Confusion and disorder reigned in these unsupervised markets; the earliest arrivals secured the best locations, unless or until forcibly ejected by stronger or tougher peddlers. Although the open air markets supplied a definite need in the community, there were many detrimental factors involved in their operation. They were unsightly, created unsanitary conditions in market streets by the deposit of garbage and waste and were a definite obstruction to traffic, as well as a fire hazard.

11. On the basis of the above passage, the MOST accurate of the following statements is:

    A. Each peddler in the original open air markets had his own fixed location.
    B. Open air markets were originally organized by means of agreements between groups of pushcart peddlers.
    C. The locations of these markets depended upon the amount of business the vendors were able to do.
    D. There was confusion and disorder in these open air markets because the peddlers were not required to pay any fees to the city.

12. Of the following, the MOST valid implication which can be made on the basis of the above passage is that the

    A. detrimental aspect of the operations of open air markets was the probable reason for the creation of enclosed markets under the supervision of the Department of Markets
    B. open air markets could not supply any community need without proper supervision
    C. original open air markets were good examples of the operation of fair competition in business
    D. possibility of obtaining a source of revenue was probably the most important reason for the city's ultimate undertaking of the supervision of open air markets

Questions 13-14.

DIRECTIONS: Questions 13 and 14 are to be answered SOLELY on the basis of the following passage.

A person who displays on his window, door, or in his place of business words or letters in Hebraic characters other than the word *kosher,* or any sign, emblem, insignia, six-pointed star, symbol or mark in simulation of same, without displaying in conjunction there-with in English letters of at least the same size as such characters, signs, emblems, insignia or marks, the words *we sell kosher meat and food only* or *we sell non-kosher meat and food only* or *we sell both kosher and non-kosher meat and food,* as the case may be, is guilty of a misdemeanor. Possession of non-kosher meat and food in any place of business advertising the sale of kosher meat and food only is presumptive evidence that the person in possession exposes the same for sale with intent to defraud, in violation of the provisions of this section.

13. Of the following, the MOST valid implication that can be made on the basis of the above passage is that a person who

    A. displays on his window a six-pointed star in addition to the word *kosher* in Hebraic letters is guilty of intent to defraud
    B. displays on his window the word *kosher* in Hebraic characters intends to indicate that he has only kosher food for sale
    C. sells both kosher and non-kosher food in the same place of business is guilty of a misdemeanor
    D. sells only that type of food which can be characterized as neither kosher nor non-kosher, such as fruit and vegetables, without an explanatory sign in English is guilty of intent to defraud

14. Of the following, the one which would constitute a violation of the rules of the above passage is a case in which a person

    A. displays the word *kosher* on his window in Hebraic letters has only kosher meat and food in the store but has some non-kosher meat in the rear of the establishment
    B. selling both kosher and non-kosher meat and food uses words in Hebraic letters, other than the word *kosher,* on his window and a sign of the same size letters in English stating *we sell both kosher and non-kosher meat and food*
    C. selling only kosher meat and food uses words in Hebraic letters, other than the word *kosher,* on his window and a sign of the same size letters in English stating *we sell kosher meat and food only*
    D. selling only non-kosher meat and food displays a six-pointed star on his window and a sign of the same size letters in English stating *we sell only non-kosher meat and food*

Questions 15-16.

DIRECTIONS: Questions 15 and 16 are to be answered SOLELY on the basis of the following passage.

COMMODITIES IN GLASS BOTTLES OR JARS

The contents of the bottle may be stated in terms of weight or of fluid measure, the weight being indicated in terms of pounds and ounces and the fluid measure being indicated in terms of gallons, quarts, pints, half-pints, gills, or fluid ounces. When contents are liquid, the amount should not be stated in terms of weight. The marking indicating content is to be on a tag attached to the bottle or upon a label. The letters shall be in bold-faced type at least one-ninth of an inch (1/9") in height for bottles or jars having a capacity of a gill, half-pint, pint, or multiples of a pint, and letters at least three-sixteenths of an inch (3/16") in height for bottles of other capacities, on a part of the tag or label free from other printing or ornamentation, leaving a clear space around the marking which indicates the contents.

15. Of the following, the one which does NOT meet the requirements of the above passage is a

    A. bottle of cooking oil with a label stating *contents—16 fluid ounces* in appropriate sized letters
    B. bottle of vinegar with a label stating *contents—8 ounces avoir.* in appropriate sized letters
    C. glass jar filled with instant coffee with a label stating *contents—1 lb. 3 ozs. avoir.* in appropriate sized letters
    D. glass jar filled with liquid bleach with a label stating *contents—1 quart* in appropriate sized letters

16. Of the following, the one which does meet the requirements of the above passage is a

    A. bottle filled with a low-calorie liquid sweetener with a label stating *contents—3 fluid ounces* in letters 1/12" high
    B. bottle filled with ammonia solution for cleaning with a label stating *contents—1 pint* in letters 1/10" high

C. jar filled with baking powder with a label stating *contents—$\frac{1}{2}$ pint* in letters $\frac{1}{4}$" high

D. jar filled with hard candy with a label stating *contents—1 lb. avoir.* in letters $\frac{1}{2}$" high

Question 17.

DIRECTIONS: Question 17 is to be answered SOLELY on the basis of the information contained in the following passage.

DEALERS IN SECOND HAND DEVICES

1. It shall be unlawful for any person to engage in or conduct the business of dealing in, trading in, selling, receiving, or repairing condemned, rebuilt, or used weighing or measuring devices without a permit therefor.

2. Such permit shall expire on the twenty-eighth day of February next succeeding the date of issuance thereof.

3. Every person engaged in the above business, within five days after the making of a repair, or the sale and delivery of a repaired, rebuilt, or used weighing or measuring device, shall serve notice in writing on the commissioner giving the name and address of the person for whom the repair has been made or to whom a repaired, rebuilt, or used weighing or measuring device has been sold or delivered, and shall include a statement that such device has been so altered, repaired, or rebuilt as to conform to the regulations of the department.

17. According to the above passage, the MOST accurate of the following statements is:

   A. A permit issued to engage in the business mentioned above, first issued on April 23, 1968, expired on February 28, 1969.
   B. A rebuilt or repaired weighing or measuring device should not operate with less error than the tolerances permitted by the regulations of the department.
   C. If a used scale in good condition is sold, it is not necessary for the seller to notify the commissioner of the name and address of the buyer.
   D. There is a difference in the time required to notify the commissioner of a repair or of a sale of a repaired device.

Questions 18-19.

DIRECTIONS: Questions 18 and 19 are to be answered SOLELY on the basis of the following passage.

A. It shall be unlawful for any person, firm, or corporation to sell or offer for sale at retail for use in internal combustion engines in motor vehicles any gasoline unless such seller shall post and keep continuously posted on the individual pump or other dispensing device from which such gasoline is sold or offered for sale a sign or placard not less than seven inches in height and eight inches in width nor larger than twelve inches in height and twelve inches in width and stating clearly in numbers of uniform size the selling price or prices per gallon of such gasoline so sold or offered for sale from such pump or other dispensing device.

B. The amount of governmental tax to be collected in connection with the sale of such gasoline shall be stated on such sign or placard and separately and apart from such selling price or prices.

18. The one of the following price signs posted on a gasoline pump which would be in violation of the above passage is a sign _____ square inches in size and _____ inches high.

    A. 144; 12   B. 84; 7   C. 72; 12   D. 60; 8

19. According to the above passage, the LEAST accurate of the following statements is:

    A. Gasoline may be sold from a dispensing device other than a pump.
    B. If two different pumps are used to sell the same grade of gasoline, a price sign must appear on each pump.
    C. The amount of governmental tax and the price of the gasoline must not be stated on the same sign.
    D. The sizes of the numbers used on a sign to indicate the price of gasoline must be the same.

Questions 20-21.

DIRECTIONS: Questions 20 and 21 are to be answered SOLELY on the basis of the following passage.

In all systems of weights and measures based on one or more arbitrary fundamental units, the concrete representation of the unit in the form of a standard is necessary, and the construction and preservation of such a standard is a matter of primary importance. Therefore, it is essential that the standard should be so constructed as to be as nearly permanent and invariable as human ingenuity can contrive. The reference of all measures to an original standard is essential for their correctness, and such a standard must be maintained and preserved in its integrity by some responsible authority which is thus able to provide against the use of false weights and measures. Accordingly, from earliest times, standards were constructed and preserved under the direction of kings and priests, and the temples were a favorite place for their deposit. Later, this duty was assumed by the government, and today we find the integrity of standards of weights and measures safeguarded by international agreement.

20. Of the following, the MOST valid implication which can be made on the basis of the above passage is that

    A. fundamental units of systems of weights and measures should be represented by quantities so constructed that they are specific and constant
    B. in the earliest times, standards were so constructed that they were as permanent and invariable as modern ones
    C. international agreement has practically relieved the U.S. government of the necessity of preserving standards of weights and measures
    D. the preservation of standards is of less importance than the ingenuity used in their construction

21. Of the following, the MOST appropriate title for the above passage is

   A. THE CONSTRUCTION AND PRESERVATION OF STANDARDS OF WEIGHTS AND MEASURES
   B. THE FIXING OF RESPONSIBILITY FOR THE ESTABLISHMENT OF STANDARDS OF WEIGHTS AND MEASURES
   C. THE HISTORY OF SYSTEMS OF WEIGHTS AND MEASURES
   D. THE VALUE OF PROPER STANDARDS IN PROVIDING CORRECT WEIGHTS AND MEASURES

Questions 22-23.

DIRECTIONS: Questions 22 and 23 are to be answered SOLELY on the basis of the following passage.

Accurate weighing and good scales insure that excess is not given just for the sake of good measure. No more striking example of the fundamental importance of correct weighing to the business man is found than in the simple and usual relation where a charge or value is obtained by multiplying a weight by a unit price. For example, a scale may weigh *light,* that is, the actual quantity delivered is in excess by 1 percent. The actual result is that the seller taxes himself. If his profit is supposed to be 10 percent of total sales, an overweight of 1 percent represents 10 percent of that profit. Under these conditions, the situation is as though the seller were required to pay a sales tax equivalent to what he is taxing himself.

22. Of the following, the MOST valid implication which can be made on the basis of the above passage is that

   A. consistent use of scales that weigh *light* will reduce sellers' profits
   B. no good businessman would give any buyer more than the weight required even if his scale is accurate
   C. the kind of situation described in the above passage could not arise if sales were being made of merchandise sold by the yard
   D. the use of incorrect scales is one of the reasons causing governments to impose sales taxes

23. According to the above passage, the MOST accurate of the following statements is:

   A. If his scale weighs *light* by an amount of 2 percent, the seller would deliver only 98 pounds when 100 pounds was the amount agreed upon.
   B. If the seller's scale weighs *heavy,* the buyer will receive an amount in excess of what he intended to purchase.
   C. If the seller's scale weighs *light* by an amount of 1 percent, a buyer who agreed to purchase 50 pounds of merchandise would actually receive $50 \frac{1}{2}$ pounds.
   D. The use of a scale which delivers an amount which is in excess of that required is an example of deliberate fraud.

Questions 24-25.

DIRECTIONS: Questions 24 and 25 are to be answered SOLELY on the basis of the following passage.

Food shall be deemed to be misbranded:
1. If its labeling is false or misleading in any particular.

2. If any word, statement, or other information required by or under authority of this article to appear on the label or labeling is not prominently placed thereon with such conspicuousness (as compared with other words, statements, designs, or devices in the labeling) and in such terms as to render it likely to be read and understood by the ordinary individual under customary conditions of purchase and use.

3. If it purports to be or is represented as a food for which a standard of quality has been prescribed and its quality falls below such standard, unless its label bears a statement that it falls below such standard.

24. According to the above passage, the MOST accurate of the following statements is:

    A. A food may be considered misbranded if the label contains a considerable amount of information which is not required.
    B. If a consumer purchased one type of canned food, although he intended to buy another, the food is probably misbranded.
    C. If a food is used in large amounts by a group of people of certain foreign origin, it can be considered misbranded unless the label is in the foreign language with which they are familiar.
    D. The required information on a label is likely to be in larger print than other information which may appear on it.

25. According to the above passage, the one of the following foods which may be considered to be misbranded is a

    A. can of peaches with a label which carries the brand name of the packer but states *Below Standard in Quality*
    B. can of vegetables with a label on which is printed a shield which states *U.S. Grade B*
    C. package of frozen food which has some pertinent information printed on it in very small type which a customer cannot read and which the store manager cannot read when asked to do so by the customer
    D. package of margarine of the same size as the usual package of butter, kept near the butter, but clearly labeled as margarine

KEY (CORRECT ANSWERS)

1.	C	11.	C
2.	D	12.	A
3.	B	13.	B
4.	B	14.	A
5.	B	15.	B
6.	A	16.	D
7.	D	17.	A
8.	C	18.	C
9.	D	19.	C
10.	A	20.	A

21. D
22. A
23. C
24. D
25. C

RECORD KEEPING
EXAMINATION SECTION
TEST 1

DIRECTIONS: Each question or incomplete statement is followed by several suggested answers or completions. Select the one that BEST answers the question or completes the statement. *PRINT THE LETTER OF THE CORRECT ANSWER IN THE SPACE AT THE RIGHT.*

Questions 1-7.

DIRECTIONS: In answering Questions 1 through 7, use the following master list. For each question, determine where the name would fit on the master list. Each answer choice indicates right before or after the name in the answer choice.

> Aaron, Jane
> Armstead, Brendan
> Bailey, Charles
> Dent, Ricardo
> Grant, Mark
> Mars, Justin
> Methieu, Justine
> Parker, Cathy
> Sampson, Suzy
> Thomas, Heather

1. Schmidt, William
   A. Right before Cathy Parker
   B. Right after Heather Thomas
   C. Right after Suzy Sampson
   D. Right before Ricardo Dent

2. Asanti, Kendall
   A. Right before Jane Aaron
   B. Right after Charles Bailey
   C. Right before Justine Methieu
   D. Right after Brendan Armstead

3. O'Brien, Daniel
   A. Right after Justine Methieu
   B. Right before Jane Aaron
   C. Right after Mark Grant
   D. Right before Suzy Sampson

4. Marrow, Alison
   A. Right before Cathy Parker
   B. Right before Justin Mars
   C. Right before Mark Grant
   D. Right after Heather Thomas

5. Grantt, Marissa
   A. Right before Mark Grant
   B. Right after Mark Grant
   C. Right after Justin Mars
   D. Right before Suzy Sampson

6. Thompson, Heath   6.____
   A. Right after Justin Mars   B. Right before Suzy Sampson
   C. Right after Heather Thomas   D. Right before Cathy Parker

DIRECTIONS: Before answering Question 7, add in all of the names from Questions 1 through 6. Then fit the name in alphabetical order based on the new list.

7. Francisco, Mildred   7.____
   A. Right before Mark Grant   B. Right after Marissa Grantt
   C. Right before Alison Marrow   D. Right after Kendall Asanti

Questions 8-10.

DIRECTIONS: In answering Questions 8 through 10, compare each pair of names and addresses. Indicate whether they are the same or different in any way.

8. William H. Pratt, J.D.   William H. Pratt, J.D.   8.____
   Attourney at Law   Attorney at Law
   A. No differences   B. 1 difference
   C. 2 differences   D. 3 differences

9. 1303 Theater Drive,; Apt. 3-B   1330 Theatre Drive,; Apt. 3-B   9.____
   A. No differences   B. 1 difference
   C. 2 differences   D. 3 differences

10. Petersdorff, Briana and Mary   Petersdorff, Briana and Mary   10.____
    A. No differences   B. 1 difference
    C. 2 differences   D. 3 differences

11. Which of the following words, if any, are misspelled?   11.____
    A. Affordable   B. Circumstansial
    C. Legalese   D. None of the above

Questions 12-13.

DIRECTIONS: Questions 12 and 13 are to be answered on the basis of the following table.

Standardized Test Results for High School Students in District #1230

	English	Math	Science	Reading
High School 1	21	22	15	18
High School 2	12	16	13	15
High School 3	16	18	21	17
High School 4	19	14	15	16

The scores for each high school in the district were averaged out and listed for each subject tested. Scores of 0-10 are significantly below College Readiness Standards. 11-15 are below College Readiness, 16-20 meet College Readiness, and 21-25 are above College Readiness.

12. If the high schools need to meet or exceed in at least half the categories in order to NOT be considered "at risk," which schools are considered "at risk"?
    A. High School 2
    B. High School 3
    C. High School 4
    D. Both A and C

12.____

13. What percentage of subjects did the district as a whole meet or exceed College Readiness standards?
    A. 25%   B. 50%   C. 75%   D. 100%

13.____

Questions 14-15.

DIRECTIONS: Questions 14 and 15 are to be answered on the basis of the following information.

You have seven employees working as a part of your team: Austin, Emily, Jeremy, Christina, Martin, Harriet, and Steve. You have just sent an e-mail informing them that there will be a mandatory training session next week. To ensure that work still gets done, you are offering the training twice during the week: once on Tuesday and also on Thursday. This way half the employees will still be working while the other half attend the training. The only other issue is that Jeremy doesn't work on Tuesdays and Harriet doesn't work on Thursdays due to compressed work schedules.

14. Which of the following is a possible attendance roster for the first training session?
    A. Emily, Jeremy, Steve
    B. Steve, Christina, Harriet
    C. Harriet, Jeremy, Austin
    D. Steve, Martin, Jeremy

14.____

15. If Harriet, Christina, and Steve attend the training session on Tuesday, which of the following is a possible roster for Thursday's training session?
    A. Jeremy, Emily, and Austin
    B. Emily, Martin, and Harriet
    C. Austin, Christina, and Emily
    D. Jeremy, Emily, and Steve

15.____

Questions 16-20.

DIRECTIONS: In answering Questions 16 through 20, you will be given a word and will need to choose the answer choice that is MOST similar or different to the word.

16. Which word means the SAME as *annual*?
    A. Monthly   B. Usually   C. Yearly   D. Constantly

16.____

17. Which word means the SAME as *effort*?
    A. Energy   B. Equate   C. Cherish   D. Commence

17.____

18. Which word means the OPPOSITE of *forlorn*?
    A. Neglected   B. Lethargy   C. Optimistic   D. Astonished

18.____

19. Which word means the SAME as *risk*?
    A. Admire   B. Hazard   C. Limit   D. Hesitant

19.____

20. Which word means the OPPOSITE of *translucent*?
    A. Opaque   B. Transparent   C. Luminous   D. Introverted

21. Last year, Jamie's annual salary was $50,000. Her boss called her today to inform her that she would receive a 20% raise for the upcoming year. How much more money will Jamie receive next year?
    A. $60,000   B. $10,000   C. $1,000   D. $51,000

22. You and a co-worker work for a temp hiring agency as part of their office staff. You both are given 6 days off per month. How many days off are you and your co-worker given in a year?
    A. 24   B. 72   C. 144   D. 48

23. If Margot makes $34,000 per year and she works 40 hours per week for all 52 weeks, what is her hourly rate?
    A. $16.34/hour   B. $17.00/hour   C. $15.54/hour   D. $13.23/hour

24. How many dimes are there in $175.00?
    A. 175   B. 1,750   C. 3,500   D. 17,500

25. If Janey is three times as old as Emily, and Emily is 3, how old is Janey?
    A. 6   B. 9   C. 12   D. 15

KEY (CORRECT ANSWERS)

1.	C		11.	B
2.	D		12.	A
3.	A		13.	D
4.	B		14.	B
5.	B		15.	A
6.	C		16.	C
7.	A		17.	A
8.	B		18.	C
9.	C		19.	B
10.	A		20.	A

21.	B
22.	C
23.	A
24.	B
25.	B

TEST 2

DIRECTIONS: Each question or incomplete statement is followed by several suggested answers or completions. Select the one that BEST answers the question or completes the statement. *PRINT THE LETTER OF THE CORRECT ANSWER IN THE SPACE AT THE RIGHT.*

Questions 1-6.

DIRECTIONS: Questions 1 through 6 are to be answered on the basis of the following information.

item	name of item to be ordered
quantity	minimum number that can be ordered
beginning amount	amount in stock at start of month
amount received	amount receiving during month
ending amount	amount in stock at end of month
amount used	amount used during month
amount to order	will need at least as much of each item as used in the previous month
unit price	cost of each unit of an item
total price	total price for the order

Item	Quantity	Beginning	Received	Ending	Amount Used	Amount to Order	Unit Price	Total Price
Pens	10	22	10	8	24	20	$0.11	$2.20
Spiral notebooks	8	30	13	12			$0.25	
Binder clips	2 boxes	3 boxes	1 box	1 box			$1.79	
Sticky notes	3 packs	12 packs	4 packs	2 packs			$1.29	
Dry erase markers	1 pack (dozen)	34 markers	8 markers	40 markers			$16.49	
Ink cartridges (printer)	1 cartridge	3 cartridges	1 cartridge	2 cartridges			$79.99	
Folders	10 folders	25 folders	15 folders	10 folders			$1.08	

1. How many packs of sticky notes were used during the month?   1.____
   A. 16   B. 10   C. 12   D. 14

2. How many folders need to be ordered for next month?   2.____
   A. 15   B. 20   C. 30   D. 40

3. What is the total price of notebooks that you will need to order?   3.____
   A. $6.00   B. $0.25   C. $4.50   D. $2.75

4. Which of the following will you spend the second most money on?   4.____
   A. Ink cartridges   B. Dry erase markers
   C. Sticky notes   D. Binder clips

5. How many packs of dry erase markers should you order?   5.____
   A. 1   B. 8   C. 12   D. 0

6. What will be the total price of the file folders you order? 6.____
   A. $20.16   B. $21.60   C. $10.80   D. $4.32

Questions 7-11.

DIRECTIONS: Questions 7 through 11 are to be answered on the basis of the following table.

Number of Car Accidents, By Location and Cause, for 2014						
	Location 1		Location 2		Location 3	
Cause	Number	Percent	Number	Percent	Number	Percent
Severe Weather	10		25		30	
Excessive Speeding	20	40	5		10	
Impaired Driving	15		15	25	8	
Miscellaneous	5		15		2	4
TOTALS	50	100	60	100	50	100

7. Which of the following is the third highest cause of accidents for all three locations? 7.____
   A. Severe Weather   B. Impaired Driving
   C. Miscellaneous   D. Excessive Speeding

8. The average number of Severe Weather accidents per week at Location 3 for the year (52 weeks) was MOST NEARLY 8.____
   A. 0.57   B. 30   C. 1   D. 1.25

9. Which location had the LARGEST percentage of accidents caused by Impaired Driving? 9.____
   A. 1   B. 2   C. 3   D. Both A and B

10. If one-third of the accidents at all three locations resulted in at least one fatality, what is the LEAST amount of deaths caused by accidents last year? 10.____
    A. 60   B. 106   C. 66   D. 53

11. What is the percentage of accidents caused by miscellaneous means from all three locations in 2014? 11.____
    A. 5%   B. 10%   C. 13%   D. 25%

12. How many pairs of the following groups of letters are exactly alike? 12.____
    ACDOBJ   ACDBOJ
    HEWBWR   HEWRWB
    DEERVS   DEERVS
    BRFQSX   BRFQSX
    WEYRVB   WEYRVB
    SPQRZA   SQRPZA

    A. 2   B. 3   C. 4   D. 5

3 (#2)

Questions 13-19.

DIRECTIONS: Questions 13 through 19 are to be answered on the basis of the following information.

In 2012, the most current information on the American population was finished. The information was compiled by 200 volunteers in each of the 50 states. The territory of Puerto Rico, a sovereign of the United States, had 25 people assigned to compile data. In February of 2010, volunteers in each state and sovereign began collecting information. In Puerto Rico, data collection finished by January 31st, 2011, while work in the United States was completed on June 30, 2012. Each volunteer gathered data on the population of their state or sovereign. When the information was compiled, volunteers sent reports to the nation's capital, Washington, D.C. Each volunteer worked 20 hours per month and put together 10 reports per month. After the data was compiled in total, 50 people reviewed the data and worked from January 2012 to December 2012.

13. How many reports were generated from February 2010 to April 2010 in Illinois and Ohio?
    A. 3,000   B. 6,000   C. 12,000   D. 15,000   13.____

14. How many volunteers in total collected population data in January 2012?
    A. 10,000   B. 2,000   C. 225   D. 200   14.____

15. How many reports were put together in May 2012?
    A. 2,000   B. 50,000   C. 100,000   D. 100,250   15.____

16. How many hours did the Puerto Rican volunteers work in the fall (September-November)?
    A. 60   B. 500   C. 1,500   D. 0   16.____

17. How many workers were compiling or reviewing data in July 2012?
    A. 25   B. 50   C. 200   D. 250   17.____

18. What was the total amount of hours worked by Nevada volunteers in July 2010?
    A. 500   B. 4,000   C. 4,500   D. 5,000   18.____

19. How many reviewers worked in January 2013?
    A. 75   B. 50   C. 0   D. 25   19.____

20. John has to file 10 documents per shelf. How many documents would it take for John to fill 40 shelves?
    A. 40   B. 400   C. 4,500   D. 5,000   20.____

21. Jill wants to travel from New York City to Los Angeles by bike, which is approximately 2,772 miles. How many miles per day would Jill need to average if she wanted to complete the trip in 4 weeks?
    A. 100   B. 89   C. 99   D. 94   21.____

4 (#2)

22. If there are 24 CPU's and only 7 monitors, how many more monitors do you need to have the same amount of monitors as CPU's? 22.____
    A. Not enough information   B. 17
    C. 31   D. 0

23. If Gerry works 5 days a week and 8 hours each day, and John works 3 days a week and 10 hours each day, how many more hours per year will Gerry work than John? 23.____
    A. They work the same amount of hours.
    B. 450
    C. 520
    D. 832

24. Jimmy gets transferred to a new office. The new office has 25 employees, but only 16 are there due to a blizzard. How many coworkers was Jimmy able to meet on his first day? 24.____
    A. 16   B. 25   C. 9   D. 7

25. If you do a fundraiser for charities in your area and raise $500 total, how much would you give to each charity if you were donating equal amounts to 3 of them? 25.____
    A. $250.00   B. $167.77   C. $50.00   D. $111.11

KEY (CORRECT ANSWERS)

1.	D		11.	C
2.	B		12.	B
3.	A		13.	C
4.	C		14.	A
5.	D		15.	C
6.	B		16.	C
7.	D		17.	B
8.	A		18.	B
9.	A		19.	C
10.	D		20.	B

21. C
22. B
23. C
24. A
25. B

TEST 3

DIRECTIONS: Each question or incomplete statement is followed by several suggested answers or completions. Select the one that BEST answers the question or completes the statement. *PRINT THE LETTER OF THE CORRECT ANSWER IN THE SPACE AT THE RIGHT.*

Questions 1-3.

DIRECTIONS: In answering Questions 1 through 3, choose the correctly spelled word.

1. A. allusion   B. alusion   C. allusien   D. allution   1.____

2. A. altitude   B. alltitude   C. atlitude   D. altlitude   2.____

3. A. althogh   B. allthough   C. althrough   D. although   3.____

Questions 4-9.

DIRECTIONS: In answering Questions 4 through 9, choose the answer that BEST completes the analogy.

4. Odometer is to mileage as compass is to   4.____
   A. speed   B. needle   C. hiking   D. direction

5. Marathon is to race as hibernation is to   5.____
   A. winter   B. dream   C. sleep   D. bear

6. Cup is to coffee as bowl is to   6.____
   A. dish   B. spoon   C. food   D. soup

7. Flow is to river as stagnant is to   7.____
   A. pool   B. rain   C. stream   D. canal

8. Paw is to cat as hoof is to   8.____
   A. lamb   B. horse   C. lion   D. elephant

9. Architect is to building as sculptor is to   9.____
   A. museum   B. chisel   C. stone   D. statue

Questions 10-14.

DIRECTIONS: Questions 10 through 14 are to be answered on the basis of the following graph.

Population of Carroll City Broken Down by Age and Gender (in Thousands)			
Age	Female	Male	Total
Under 15	60	60	120
15-23		22	
24-33		20	44
34-43	13	18	31
44-53	20		67
64 and Over	65	65	130
TOTAL	230	232	462

10. How many people in the city are between the ages of 15-23?
    A. 70   B. 46,000   C. 70,000   D. 225,000

11. Approximately what percentage of the total population of the city was female aged 24-33?
    A. 10%   B. 5%   C. 15%   D. 25%

12. If 33% of the males have a job and 55% of females don't have a job, which of the following statements is TRUE?
    A. Males have approximately 2,600 more jobs than females.
    B. Females have approximately 49,000 more jobs than males.
    C. Females have approximately 26,000 more jobs than males.
    D. None of the above statements are true.

13. How many females between the ages of 15-23 live in Carroll City?
    A. 67,000   B. 24,000   C. 48,000   D. 91,000

14. Assume all males 44-53 living in Carroll City are employed. If two-thirds of males age 44-53 work jobs outside of Carroll City, how many work within city limits?
    A. 31,333
    B. 15,667
    C. 47,000
    D. Cannot answer the question with the information provided

Questions 15-16.

DIRECTIONS: Questions 15 and 16 are labeled as shown. Alphabetize them for filing. Choose the answer that correctly shows the order.

15. (1) AED
    (2) OOS
    (3) FOA
    (4) DOM
    (5) COB

    A. 2-5-4-3-2   B. 1-4-5-2-3   C. 1-5-4-2-3   D. 1-5-4-3-2

16. Alphabetize the names of the people. Last names are given last.
    (1) Lindsey Jamestown
    (2) Jane Alberta
    (3) Ally Jamestown
    (4) Allison Johnston
    (5) Lyle Moreno

    A. 2-1-3-4-5   B. 3-4-2-1-5   C. 2-3-1-4-5   D. 4-3-2-1-5

17. Which of the following words is misspelled?
    A. disgust
    B. whisper
    C. locale
    D. none of the above

Questions 18-21.

DIRECTIONS: Questions 18 through 21 are to be answered on the basis of the following list of employees.

    Robertson, Aaron
    Bacon, Gina
    Jerimiah, Trace
    Gillette, Stanley
    Jacks, Sharon

18. Which employee name would come in third in alphabetized list?
    A. Robertson, Aaron
    B. Jerimiah, Trace
    C. Gillette, Stanley
    D. Jacks, Sharon

19. Which employee's first name starts with the letter in the alphabet that is five letters after the first letter of their last name?
    A. Jerimiah, Trace
    B. Bacon, Gina
    C. Jacks, Sharon
    D. Gillette, Stanley

20. How many employees have last names that are exactly five letters long?
    A. 1   B. 2   C. 3   D. 4

4 (#3)

21. How many of the employees have either a first or last name that starts with the letter "G"?
 A. 1 B. 2 C. 4 D. 5

Questions 22-25.

DIRECTIONS: Questions 22 through 25 are to be answered on the basis of the following chart.

Bicycle Sales (Model #34JA32)							
Country	May	June	July	August	September	October	Total
Germany	34	47	45	54	56	60	296
Britain	40	44	36	47	47	46	260
Ireland	37	32	32	32	34	33	200
Portugal	14	14	14	16	17	14	89
Italy	29	29	28	31	29	31	177
Belgium	22	24	24	26	25	23	144
Total	176	198	179	206	208	207	1166

22. What percentage of the overall total was sold to the German importer?
 A. 25.3% B. 22% C. 24.1% D. 23%

23. What percentage of the overall total was sold in September?
 A. 24.1% B. 25.6% C. 17.9% D. 24.6%

24. What is the average number of units per month imported into Belgium over the first four months shown?
 A. 26 B. 20 C. 24 D. 31

25. If you look at the three smallest importers, what is their total import percentage?
 A. 35.1% B. 37.1% C. 40% D. 28%

KEY (CORRECT ANSWERS)

1.	A	11.	B
2.	A	12.	C
3.	D	13.	C
4.	D	14.	B
5.	C	15.	D
6.	D	16.	C
7.	A	17.	D
8.	B	18.	D
9.	D	19.	B
10.	C	20.	B

21.	B
22.	A
23.	C
24.	C
25.	A

TEST 4

DIRECTIONS: Each question or incomplete statement is followed by several suggested answers or completions. Select the one that BEST answers the question or completes the statement. *PRINT THE LETTER OF THE CORRECT ANSWER IN THE SPACE AT THE RIGHT.*

Questions 1-6.

DIRECTIONS: In answering Questions 1 through 6, choose the sentence that represents the BEST example of English grammar.

1. A. Joey and me want to go on a vacation next week. 1.____
   B. Gary told Jim he would need to take some time off.
   C. If turning six years old, Jim's uncle would teach Spanish to him.
   D. Fax a copy of your resume to Ms. Perez and me.

2. A. Jerry stood in line for almost two hours. 2.____
   B. The reaction to my engagement was less exciting than I thought it would be.
   C. Carlos and me have done great work on this project.
   D. Two parts of the speech needs to be revised before tomorrow.

3. A. Arriving home, the alarm was tripped. 3.____
   B. Jonny is regarded as a stand up guy, a responsible parent, and he doesn't give up until a task is finished.
   C. Each employee must submit a drug test each month.
   D. One of the documents was incinerated in the explosion.

4. A. As soon as my parents get home, I told them I finished all of my chores. 4.____
   B. I asked my teacher to send me my missing work, check my absences, and how did I do on my test.
   C. Matt attempted to keep it concealed from Jenny and me.
   D. If Mary or him cannot get work done on time, I will have to split them up.

5. A. Driving to work, the traffic report warned him of an accident on Highway 47. 5.____
   B. Jimmy has performed well this season.
   C. Since finishing her degree, several job offers have been given to Cam.
   D. Our boss is creating unstable conditions for we employees.

6. A. The thief was described as a tall man with a wiry mustache weighing approximately 150 pounds. 6.____
   B. She gave Patrick and I some more time to finish our work.
   C. One of the books that he ordered was damaged in shipping.
   D. While talking on the rotary phone, the car Jim was driving skidded off the road.

Questions 7-9.

DIRECTIONS: Questions 7 through 9 are to be answered on the basis of the following graph.

Ice Lake Frozen Flight (2002-2013)		
Year	Number of Participants	Temperature (Fahrenheit)
2002	22	4°
2003	50	33°
2004	69	18°
2005	104	22°
2006	108	24°
2007	288	33°
2008	173	9°
2009	598	39°
2010	698	26°
2011	696	30°
2012	777	28°
2013	578	32°

7. Which two year span had the LARGEST difference between temperatures?
   A. 2002 and 2003
   B. 2011 and 2012
   C. 2008 and 2009
   D. 2003 and 2004

8. How many total people participated in the years after the temperature reached at least 29°?
   A. 2,295   B. 1,717   C. 2,210   D. 4,543

9. In 2007, the event saw 288 participants, while in 2008 that number dropped to 173. Which of the following reasons BEST explains the drop in participants?
   A. The event had not been going on that long and people didn't know about it.
   B. The lake water wasn't cold enough to have people jump in.
   C. The temperature was too cold for many people who would have normally participated.
   D. None of the above reasons explain the drop in participants.

10. In the following list of numbers, how many times does 4 come just after 2 when 2 comes just after an odd number?
    2365247653898632488572486392424
    A. 2   B. 3   C. 4   D. 5

11. Which choice below lists the letter that is as far after B as S is after N in the alphabet?
    A. G   B. H   C. I   D. J

Questions 12-15.

DIRECTIONS: Questions 12 through 15 are to be answered on the basis of the following directory and list of changes.

Directory		
Name	Emp. Type	Position
Julie Taylor	Warehouse	Packer
James King	Office	Administrative Assistant
John Williams	Office	Salesperson
Ray Moore	Warehouse	Maintenance
Kathleen Byrne	Warehouse	Supervisor
Amy Jones	Office	Salesperson
Paul Jonas	Office	Salesperson
Lisa Wong	Warehouse	Loader
Eugene Lee	Office	Accountant
Bruce Lavine	Office	Manager
Adam Gates	Warehouse	Packer
Will Suter	Warehouse	Packer
Gary Lorper	Office	Accountant
Jon Adams	Office	Salesperson
Susannah Harper	Office	Salesperson

Directory Updates:
- Employee e-mail addresses will adhere to the following guidelines: lastnamefirstname@apexindustries.com (ex. Susannah Harper is harpersusannah@apexindustries.com). Currently, employees in the warehouse share one e-mail, distribution@apexindustries.com.
- The "Loader" position will now be referred to as "Specialist I"
- Adam Gates has accepted a Supervisor position within the Warehouse and is no longer a Packer. All warehouse employees report to the two Supervisors and all office employees report to the Manager.

12. Amy Jones tried to send an e-mail to Adam Gates, but it wouldn't send. 12.____
    Which of the following offers the BEST explanation?
    A. Amy put Adam's first name first and then his last name.
    B. Adam doesn't check his e-mail, so he wouldn't know if he received the e-mail or not.
    C. Adam does not have his own e-mail.
    D. Office employees are not allowed to send e-mails to each other.

13. How many Packers currently work for Apex Industries? 13.____
    A. 2   B. 3   C. 4   D. 5

14. What position does Lisa Wong currently hold? 14.____
    A. Specialist I   B. Secretary
    C. Administrative Assistant   D. Loader

15. If an employee wanted to contact the office manager, which of the following e-mails should the e-mail be sent to?
    A. officemanager@apexindustries.com
    B. brucelavine@apexindustries.com
    C. lavinebruce@apexindustries.com
    D. distribution@apexindustries.com

15.____

Questions 16-19.

DIRECTIONS: In answering Questions 16 through 19, compare the three names, numbers or addresses.

16. Smiley Yarnell   Smiley Yarnel   Smily Yarnell   16.____
    A. All three are exactly alike.
    B. The first and second are exactly alike.
    C. The second and third are exactly alike.
    D. All three are different.

17. 1583 Theater Drive   1583 Theater Drive   1583 Theatre Drive   17.____
    A. All three are exactly alike.
    B. The first and second are exactly alike.
    C. The second and third are exactly alike.
    D. All three are different.

18. 3341893212   3341893212   3341893212   18.____
    A. All three are exactly alike.
    B. The first and second are exactly alike.
    C. The second and third are exactly alike.
    D. All three are different.

19. Douglass Watkins   Douglas Watkins   Douglass Watkins   19.____
    A. All three are exactly alike.
    B. The first and third are exactly alike.
    C. The second and third are exactly alike.
    D. All three are different.

Questions 20-24.

DIRECTIONS: In answering Questions 20 through 24, you will be presented with a word. Choose the synonym that BEST represents the word in question.

20. Flexible
    A. delicate   B. inflammable   C. strong   D. pliable

20.____

21. Alternative
    A. choice   B. moderate   C. lazy   D. value

21.____

22. Corroborate
    A. examine   B. explain   C. verify   D. explain

23. Respiration
    A. recovery   B. breathing   C. sweating   D. selfish

24. Negligent
    A. lazy   B. moderate   C. hopeless   D. lax

25. Plumber is to Wrench as Painter is to
    A. pipe   B. shop   C. hammer   D. brush

KEY (CORRECT ANSWERS)

1. D
2. A
3. D
4. C
5. B

6. C
7. C
8. B
9. C
10. C

11. A
12. C
13. A
14. A
15. C

16. D
17. B
18. A
19. B
20. D

21. A
22. C
23. B
24. D
25. D

PREPARING WRITTEN MATERIAL

PARAGRAPH REARRANGEMENT
COMMENTARY

The sentences that follow are in scrambled order. You are to rearrange them in proper order and indicate the letter choice containing the correct answer at the space at the right.

Each group of sentences in this section is actually a paragraph presented in scrambled order. Each sentence in the group has a place in that paragraph; no sentence is to be left out. You are to read each group of sentences and decide upon the best order in which to put the sentences so as to form a well-organized paragraph.

The questions in this section measure the ability to solve a problem when all the facts relevant to its solution are not given.

More specifically, certain positions of responsibility and authority require the employee to discover connection between events sometimes, apparently, unrelated. In order to do this, the employee will find it necessary to correctly infer that unspecified events have probably occurred or are likely to occur. This ability becomes especially important when action must be taken on incomplete information.

Accordingly, these questions require competitors to choose among several suggested alternatives, each of which presents a different sequential arrangement of the events. Competitors must choose the MOST logical of the suggested sequences.

In order to do so, they may be required to draw on general knowledge to infer missing concepts or events that are essential to sequencing the given events. Competitors should be careful to infer only what is essential to the sequence. The plausibility of the wrong alternatives will always require the inclusion of unlikely events or of additional chains of events which are NOT essential to sequencing the given events.

It's very important to remember that you are looking for the best of the four possible choices, and that the best choice of all may not even be one of the answers you're given to choose from.

There is no one right way to solve these problems. Many people have found it helpful to first write out the order of the sentences, as they would have arranged them, on their scrap paper before looking at the possible answers. If their optimum answer is there, this can save them some time. If it isn't, this method can still give insight into solving the problem. Others find it most helpful to just go through each of the possible choices, contrasting each as they go along. You should use whatever method feels comfortable and works for you.

While most of these types of questions are not that difficult, we've added a higher percentage of the difficult type, just to give you more practice. Usually there are only one or two questions on this section that contain such subtle distinctions that you're unable to answer confidently. And you then may find yourself stuck deciding between two possible choices, neither of which you're sure about.

PREPARING WRITTEN MATERIAL
PARAGRAPH REARRANGEMENT
EXAMINATION SECTION
TEST 1

DIRECTIONS: The sentences that follow are in scrambled order. You are to rearrange them in proper order and indicate the letter choice containing the CORRECT answer. *PRINT THE LETTER OF THE CORRECT ANSWER IN THE SPACE AT THE RIGHT.*

1. Police Officer Jenner responds to the scene of a burglary at 2106 La Vista Boulevard. He is approached by an elderly man named Richard Jenkins, whose account of the incident includes the following five sentences:
    I. I saw that the lock on my apartment door had been smashed and the door was open.
    II. My apartment was a shambles; my belongings were everywhere and my television set was missing.
    III. As I walked down the hallway toward the bedroom, I heard someone opening a window.
    IV. I left work at 5:30 P.M. and took the bus home.
    V. At that time, I called the police.
    The MOST logical order for the above sentence to appear in the report is
    A. I, V, IV, II, III   B. IV, I, II, III, V   C. I, V, II, III, IV   D. IV, III, II, V, I

    1.____

2. Police Officer LaJolla is writing an Incident Report in which back-up assistance was required. The report will contain the following five sentences:
    I. The radio dispatcher asked what my location was and he then dispatched patrol cars for back-up assistance.
    II. At approximately 9:30 P.M., while I was walking my assigned footpost, a gunman fired three shots at me.
    III. I quickly turned around and saw a white male, approximately 5'10", with black hair, wearing blue jeans, a yellow T-shirt, and white sneaker, running across the avenue carrying a handgun.
    IV. When the back-up officers arrived, we searched the area but could not find the suspect.
    V. I advised the radio dispatcher that a gunman had just fired a gun at me, and then I gave the dispatcher a description of the man
    The MOST logical order for the above sentences to appear in the report is:
    A. III, V, II, IV, I   B. II, III, V, I, IV   C. III, II, IV, I, V   D. II, V, I, III, IV

    2.____

3. Police Officer Durant is completing a report of a robbery and assault. The report will contain the following five sentences:
    I. I went to Mount Snow Hospital to interview a man who was attacked and robbed of his wallet earlier that night.
    II. An ambulance arrived at 82nd Street and 3rd Avenue and took an intoxicated, wounded man to Mount Snow Hospital
    III. Two youths attacked the man and stole his wallet.

    3.____

IV. A well-dressed man left Hanratty's Bar very drunk, with his wallet hanging out of his back pocket.
V. A passerby dialed 911 and requested police and ambulance assistance.

The MOST logical order for the above sentences to appear in the report is
A. I, II, IV, III, V   B. IV, III, V, II, I   C. IV, V, II, III, I   D. V, IV, III, II, I

4. Police Officer Boswell is preparing a report of an armed robbery and assault which will contain the following five sentences:
   I. Both men approached the bartender and one of them drew a gun.
   II. The bartender immediately went to grab the phone at the bar.
   III. One of the men leaped over the counter and smashed a bottle over the bartender's head.
   IV. Two men in a blue Buick drove up to the bar and went inside.
   V. I found the cash register empty and the bartender unconscious on the floor, with the phone still dangling off the hook.

   The MOST logical order for the above sentences to appear in the report is
   A. IV, I, II, II, V   B. V, IV, III, I, II   C. IV, III, II, V, I   D. II, I, III, IV, V

5. Police Officer Mitzler is preparing a report of a bank robbery, which will contain the following five sentences:
   I. The teller complied with the instructions on the note, but also hit the silent alarm.
   II. The perpetrator then fled south on Broadway.
   III. A suspicious male entered the bank at approximately 10:45 A.M.
   IV. At this time, an undetermined amount of money has been taken.
   V. He approached the teller on the far right side and handed her a note.

   The MOST logical order for the above sentences to appear in the report is:
   A. III, V, I, II, IV   B. I, III, V, II, IV   C. III, V, IV, I, II   D. III, V, II, IV, I

6. A Police Officer is preparing an Accident Report for an accident which occurred at the intersection of East 119th Street and Lexington Avenue. The report will include the following five sentences:
   I. On September 18, while driving ten children to school, a school bus driver passed out.
   II. Upon arriving at the scene, I notified the dispatcher to send an ambulance.
   III. I notified the parents of each child once I got to the station house.
   IV. He said the school bus, while traveling west on East 119th Street, struck a parked Ford which was on the southwest corner of East 119th Street.
   V. A witness by the name of John Ramos came up to me to describe what happened.

   The MOST logical order for the above sentences to appear in the Accident Report is:
   A. I, II, V, III, IV   B. I, II, V, IV, III   C. II, V, I, III, IV   D. II, V, I, IV, III

7. A Police Officer is preparing a report concerning a dispute. The report will contain the following five sentences:
   I. The passenger got out of the back of the taxi and leaned through the front window to complain to the driver about the fare.

II. The driver of the taxi caught up with the passenger and knocked him to the ground; the passenger then kicked the driver and a scuffle ensued.
III. The taxi drew up in front of the high-rise building and stopped.
IV. The driver got out of the taxi and followed the passenger into the lobby of the apartment building.
V. The doorman tried but was unable to break up the fight, at which point he called the precinct.

The MOST logical order for the above sentences to appear in the report is
    A. III, I, IV, II, V   B. III, IV, I, II, V   C. III, IV, II, V, I   D. V, I, III, IV, II

8. Police Officer Morrow is writing an Incident Report. The report will include the following four sentences:
   I. The man reached into his pocket and pulled out a gun.
   II. While on foot patrol, I identified a suspect, who was wanted for six robberies in the area, from a wanted picture I was carrying.
   III. I drew my weapon and fired six rounds at the suspect, killing him instantly.
   IV. I called for back-up assistance and told the man to put his hands up.

   The MOST logical order for the above sentences to appear in the report is
       A. II, III, IV, I   B. IV, I, III, II   C. IV, I, II, III   D. II, IV, I, III

9. Sergeant Allen responds to a call at 16 Grove Street regarding a missing child. At the scene, the Sergeant is met by Police Officer Samuels, who gives a brief account of the incident consisting of the following five sentences:
   I. I transmitted the description and waited for you to arrive before I began searching the area.
   II. Mrs. Banks, the mother, reports that she last saw her daughter Julie about 7:30 A.M. when she took her to school.
   III. About 6 P.M., my partner and I arrived at this location to investigate a report of a missing 8-year-old girl.
   IV. When Mrs. Banks left her, Julie was wearing a red and white striped T-shirt, blue jeans, and white sneakers.
   V. Mrs. Banks dropped her off in front of the playground of P.S. 11.

   The MOST logical order for the above sentences to appear in the report is
       A. III, V, IV, II, I   B. III, II, V, IV, I   C. III, IV, I, II, V   D. III, II, IV, I, V

10. Police Officer Franco is completing a report of an assault. The report will contain the following five sentences:
    I. In the park I observed an elderly man lying on the ground, bleeding from a back wound.
    II. I applied first aid to control the bleeding and radioed for an ambulance to respond.
    III. The elderly man stated that he was sitting on the park bench when he was attacked from behind by two males.
    IV. I received a report of a man's screams coming from inside the park, and I went to investigate.
    V. The old man could not give a description of his attackers.

    The MOST logical order for the above sentences to appear in the report is
        A. IV, I, II, III, V   B. V, III, I, IV, II   C. IV, III, V, II, I   D. II, I, V, IV, III

11. Police Officer Williams is completing a Crime Report. The report contains the following five sentences:
    I. As Police Officer Hanson and I approached the store, we noticed that the front door was broken.
    II. After determining that the burglars had fled, we notified the precinct of the burglary.
    III. I walked through the front door as Police Officer Hanson walked around to the back.
    IV. At approximately midnight, an alarm was heard at the Apex Jewelry Store.
    V. We searched the store and found no one.
    The MOST logical order for the above sentences to appear in the report is
    A. I, IV, II, III, V   B. I, IV, III, V, II   C. IV, I, III, II, V   D. IV, I, III, V, II

11.____

12. Police Officer Clay is giving a report to the news media regarding someone who has jumped from the Empire State Building. His report will include the following five sentences:
    I. I responded to the 86th floor, where I found the person at the edge of the roof.
    II. A security guard at the building had reported that a man was on the roof at the 86th floor.
    III. At 5:30 P.M., the person jumped from the building.
    IV. I received a call from the radio dispatcher at 4:50 P.M. to respond to the Empire State Building.
    V. I tried to talk to the person and convince him not to jump.
    The MOST logical order for the above sentences to appear in the report is
    A. I, II, IV, III, V   B. III, IV, I, II, V   C. II, IV, I, III, V   D. IV, II, I, V, III

12.____

13. The following five sentences are part of a report of a burglary written by Police Officer Reed:
    I. When I arrived at 2400 1st Avenue, I noticed that the door was slightly open.
    II. I yelled out, *Police, don't move!*
    III. As I entered the apartment, I saw a man with a TV set passing through a window to another man standing on a fire escape.
    IV. While on foot patrol, I was informed by the radio dispatcher that a burglary was in progress at 2400 1st Avenue.
    V. However, the burglars quickly ran down the fire escape.
    The MOST logical order for the above sentences to appear in the report is
    A. I, III, IV, V, II   B. IV, I, III, V, II   C. IV, I, III, II, V   D. I, IV, III, II, V

13.____

14. Police Officer Jenkins is preparing a report for Lost or Stolen Property. The report will include the following five sentences:
    I. On the stairs, Mr. Harris slipped on a wet leaf and fell on the landing.
    II. It wasn't until he got to the token booth that Mr. Harris realized his wallet was no longer in his back pants pocket.
    III. A boy wearing a football jersey helped him up and brushed off the back of Mr. Harris' pants.
    IV. Mr. Harris states he was walking up the stairs to the elevated subway at Queensborough Plaza.
    V. Before Mr. Harris could thank him, the boy was running down the stairs to the street.

14.____

The MOST logical order for the above sentences to appear in the report is
A. IV, III, V, I, II   B. IV, I, III, V, II   C. I, IV, II, III, V   D. I, II, IV, III, V

15. Police Officer Hubbard is completing a report of a missing person. The report will contain the following five sentences:
    I. I visited the store at 7:55 P.M. and asked the employees if they had seen a girl fitting the description I had been given.
    II. She gave me a description and said she had gone into the local grocery store at about 6:15 P.M.
    III. I asked the woman for a description of her daughter.
    IV. The distraught woman called the precinct to report that her daughter, aged 12, had not returned from an errand.
    V. The storekeeper said a girl matching the description had been in the store earlier, but he could not give an exact time.
    The MOST logical order for the above sentences to appear in the report is
    A. I, III, II, V, IV   B. IV, III, II, I, V   C. V, I, II, III, IV   D. III, I, II, IV, V

16. A police officer is completing an entry in his Daily Activity Log regarding traffic summonses which he issued. The following five sentences will be included in the entry:
    I. I was on routine patrol parked 16 yards west of 170th Street and Clay Avenue.
    II. The summonses were issued for unlicensed operator and disobeying a steady red light.
    III. At 8 A.M. hours, I observed an auto traveling westbound on 170th Street not stop for a steady red light at the intersection of Clay Avenue and 170th Street.
    IV. I stopped the driver of the auto and determined that he did not have a valid driver's license.
    V. After a brief conversation, I informed the motorist that he was receiving two summonses.
    The MOST logical order for the above sentences to appear in the report is
    A. I, III, IV, V, II   B. III, IV, II, V, I   C. V, II, I, III, IV   D. IV, V, II, I, III

17. The following sentences appeared on an Incident Report:
    I. Three teenagers who had been ejected from the theater were yelling at patrons who were now entering.
    II. Police Officer Dixon told the teenagers to leave the area.
    III. The teenager said that they were told by the manager to leave the theater because they were talking during the movie.
    IV. The theater manager called the precinct at 10:20 P.M. to report a disturbance outside the theater.
    V. A patrol car responded to the theater at 10:42 P.M. and two police officers went over to the teenagers.
    The MOST logical order for the above sentences to appear in the Incident Report is
    A. I, V, IV, III, II   B. IV, I, V, III, II   C. IV, I, III, V, II   D. IV, III, I, V, II

18. Activity Log entries are completed by police officers. Police Officer Samuels has written an entry concerning vandalism and part of it contains the following five sentences:
    I. The man, in his early twenties, ran down the block and around the corner.
    II. A man passing the store threw a brick through a window of the store.
    III. I arrived on the scene and began to question the witnesses about the incident.
    IV. Malcolm Holmes, the owner of the Fast Service Shoe Repair Store, was working in the back of the store at approximately 3 P.M.
    V. After the man fled, Mr. Holmes called the police.
    The MOST logical order for the above sentences to appear in the Activity Log is
    A. IV, II, I, V, III   B. II, IV, I, III, V   C. II, I, IV, III, V   D. IV, II, V, III, I

18.____

19. Police Officer Buckley is preparing a report concerning a dispute in a restaurant. The report will contain the following five sentences:
    I. The manager, Charles Chin, and a customer, Edward Green, were standing near the register arguing over the bill.
    II. The manager refused to press any charges providing Green pay the check and leave.
    III. While on foot patrol, I was informed by a passerby of a disturbance in the Dragon Flame Restaurant.
    IV. Green paid the $15.00 check and left the restaurant.
    V. According to witnesses, the customer punched the owner in the face when Chin asked him for the amount due.
    The MOST logical order for the above sentences to appear in the report is
    A. III, I, V, II, IV   B. I, II, III, IV, V   C. V, I, III, II, IV   D. III, V, II, IV, I

19.____

20. Police Officer Wilkins is preparing a report for leaving the scene of an accident. The report will include the following five sentences:
    I. The Dodge struck the right rear fender of Mrs. Smith's 2010 Ford and continued on its way.
    II. Mrs. Smith stated she was making a left turn from 40th Street onto Third Avenue.
    III. As the car passed, Mrs. Smith noticed the dangling rear license plate #412AEJ.
    IV. Mrs. Smith complained to police of back pains and was removed by ambulance to Bellevue Hospital.
    V. An old green Dodge traveling up Third Avenue went through the red light at 40th Street and Third Avenue.
    The MOST logical order for the above sentences to appear in the report is
    A. V, III, I, II, IV   B. I, III, II, V, IV   C. IV, V, I, II, III   D. II, V, I, III, IV

20.____

21. Detective Simon is completing a Crime Report. The report contains the following five sentences:
    I. Police Officer Chin, while on foot patrol, heard the yelling and ran in the direction of the man.
    II. The man, carrying a large hunting knife, left the High Sierra Sporting Goods Store at approximately 10:30 A.M.

21.____

III. When the man heard Police Officer Chin, he stopped, dropped the knife, and began to cry.
IV. As Police Officer Chin approached the man, he drew his gun and yelled, *Police, freeze.*
V. After the man left the store, he began yelling, over and over, *I am going to kill myself!*

The MOST logical order for the above sentences to appear in the report is
   A. V, II, I, IV, III   B. II, V, I, IV, III   C. II, V, IV, I, III   D. II, I, V, IV, III

22. Police Officer Miller is preparing a Complaint Report which will include the following five sentences:
   I. From across the lot, he yelled to the boys to get away from his car.
   II. When he came out of the store, he noticed two teenage boys trying to break into his car.
   III. The boys fled as Mr. Johnson ran to his car.
   IV. Mr. Johnson stated that he parked his car in the municipal lot behind Tams Department Store.
   V. Mr. Johnson saw that the door lock had been broken, but nothing was missing from inside the auto.

   The MOST logical order for the above sentences to appear in the report is
      A. IV, I, II, V, III   B. II, III, I, V, IV   C. IV, II, I, III, V   D. I, II, III, V, IV

23. Police Officer O'Hara completes a Universal Summons for a motorist who has just passed a red traffic light. The Universal Summons includes the following five sentences:
   I. As the car passed the light, I followed in the patrol car.
   II. After the driver stopped the car, he stated that the light was yellow, not red.
   III. A blue Cadillac sedan passed the red light on the corner of 79th Street and 3rd Avenue at 11:25 P.M.
   IV. As a result, the driver was informed that he did pass a red light and that his brake lights were not working.
   V. The driver in the Cadillac stopped his car as soon as he saw the patrol car, and I noticed that the brake lights were not working.

   The MOST logical order for the above sentences to appear in the Universal Summons is
      A. I, III, V, II, IV   B. III, I, V, II, IV   C. III, I, V, IV, II   D. I, III, IV, II, V

24. Detective Egan is preparing a follow-up report regarding a homicide on 170th Street and College Avenue. An unknown male was found at the scene. The report will contain the following five sentences:
   I. Police Officer Gregory wrote down the names, addresses, and phone numbers of the witnesses.
   II. A 911 operator received a call of a man shot and dispatched Police Officers Worth and Gregory to the scene.
   III. They discovered an unidentified male dead on the street.
   IV. Police Officer Worth notified the Precinct Detective Unit immediately.
   V. At approximately 9:00 A.M., an unidentified male shot another male in the chest during an argument.

The MOST logical order for the above sentences to appear in the report is
A. V, II, III, IV, I B. II, III, V, IV, I C. IV, I, V, II, III D. V, III, II, IV, I

25. Police Officer Tracey is preparing a Robbery Report which will include the following five sentences:
I. I ran around the corner and observe a man pointing a gun at a taxidriver.
II. I informed the man I was a police officer and that he should not move.
III. I was on the corner of 125th Street and Park Avenue when I heard a scream coming from around the corner.
IV. The man turned around and fired one shot at me.
V. I fired once, shooting him in the arm and causing him to fall to the ground.
The MOST logical order for the above sentences to appear in the report is
A. I, III, IV, II, V B. IV, V, II, I, III C. III, I, II, IV, V D. III, I, V, II, IV

KEY (CORRECT ANSWERS)

1.	B	11.	D
2.	B	12.	D
3.	B	13.	C
4.	A	14.	B
5.	A	15.	B
6.	B	16.	A
7.	A	17.	B
8.	D	18.	A
9.	B	19.	A
10.	A	20.	D

21.	B
22.	C
23.	B
24.	A
25.	C

TEST 2

DIRECTIONS: The sentences that follow are in scrambled order. You are to rearrange them in proper order and indicate the letter choice containing the CORRECT answer. *PRINT THE LETTER OF THE CORRECT ANSWER IN THE SPACE AT THE RIGHT*

1. Police Officer Weiker is completing a Complaint Report which will contain the following five sentences:
   I. Mr. Texlor was informed that the owner of the van would receive a parking ticket and that the van would be towed away.
   II. The police tow truck arrived approximately one half hour after Mr. Texlor complained.
   III. While on foot patrol on West End Avenue, I saw the owner of Rand's Restaurant arrive to open his business.
   IV. Mr. Texlor, the owner, called to me and complained that he could not receive deliveries because a van was blocking his driveway.
   V. The van's owner later reported to the precinct that his van had been stolen, and he was then informed that it had been towed.
   The MOST logical order for the above sentences to appear in the report is
   A. III, V, I, II, IV B. III, IV, I, II, V C. IV, III, I, II, V D. IV, III, II, I, V

   1.____

2. Police Officer Ames is completing an entry in his Activity Log. The entry contains the following five sentences:
   I. Mr. Sands gave me a complete description of the robber.
   II. Alvin Sands, owner of the Star Delicatessen, called the precinct to report he had just been robbed.
   III. I then notified all police patrol vehicles to look for a white male in his early twenties wearing brown pants and shirt, a black leather jacket, and black and white sneakers.
   IV. I arrived on the scene after being notified by the precinct that a robbery had just occurred at the Star Delicatessen.
   V. Twenty minutes later, a man fitting the description was arrested by a police officer on patrol six blocks from the delicatessen.
   The MOST logical order for the above sentences to appear in the Activity Log is
   A. II, I, IV, III, V B. II IV, III, I, V C. II, IV, I, III, V D. II, IV, I, V, III

   2.____

3. Police Officer Benson is completing a Complaint Report concerning a stolen taxicab, which will include the following five sentences:
   I. Police Officer Benson noticed that a cab was parked next to a fire hydrant.
   II. Dawson *borrowed* the cab for transportation purposes since he was in a hurry.
   III. Ed Dawson got into his car and tried to start it, but the battery was dead.
   IV. When he reached his destination, he parked the cab by a fire hydrant and placed the keys under the seat.
   V. He looked around and saw an empty cab with the engine running.
   The MOST logical order for the above sentences to appear in the report is
   A. I, III, II, IV, V B. III, I, II, V, IV C. III, V, II, IV, I D. V, II, IV, III, I

   3.____

4. Police Officer Hatfield is reviewing his Activity Log entry prior to completing a report. The entry contains the following five sentences:
   I. When I arrived at Zand's Jewelry Store, I noticed that the door was slightly open.
   II. I told the burglar I was a police officer and that he should stand still or he would be shot.
   III. As I entered the store, I saw a man wearing a ski mask attempting to open the safe in the back of the store.
   IV. On December 16, 2020, at 1:38 A.M., I was informed that a burglary was in progress at Zand's Jewelry Store on East 59th Street.
   V. The burglar quickly pulled a knife from his pocket when he saw me.
   The MOST logical order for the above sentences to appear in the report is
      A. IV, I, III, V, II   B. I, IV, III, V, II   C. IV, III, II, V, I   D. I, III, IV, V, II

4.____

5. Police Officer Lorenz is completing a report of a murder. The report will contain the following five statements made by a witness:
   I. I was awakened by the sound of a gunshot coming from the apartment next door and I decided to check.
   II. I entered the apartment and looked into the kitchen and the bathroom.
   III. I found Mr. Hubbard's body slumped in the bathtub.
   IV. The door to the apartment was open, but I didn't see anyone.
   V. He had been shot in the head.
   The MOST logical order for the above sentences to appear in the report is
      A. I, III, II, IV, V   B. I, IV, II, III, V   C. IV, II, I, III, V   D. III, I, II, IV, V

5.____

6. Police Officer Baldwin is preparing an accident report which will include the following five sentences:
   I. The old man lay on the ground for a few minutes, but was not physically hurt.
   II. Charlie Watson, a construction worker, was repairing some brick work at the top of a building at 54th Street and Madison Avenue.
   III. Steven Green, his partner, warned him that this could be dangerous, but Watson ignored him.
   IV. A few minutes later, one of the bricks thrown by Watson smashed to the ground in front of an old man, who fainted out of fright.
   V. Mr. Watson began throwing some of the bricks over the side of the building.
   The MOST logical order for the above sentences to appear in the report is
      A. II, V, III, IV, I   B. I, IV, II, V, III   C. III, II, IV, V, I   D. II, III, I, IV, V

6.____

7. Police Officer Porter is completing an Incident Report concerning her rescue of a woman being held hostage by a former boyfriend. Her report will contain the following five sentences:
   I. I saw a man holding .25 caliber gun to a woman's head, but he did not see me.
   II. I then broke a window and gained access to the house.
   III. As I approached the house on foot, a gunshot rang out and I heard a woman scream.
   IV. A decoy van brought me as close as possible to the house where the woman was being held hostage.

7.____

V. I ordered the man to drop his gun, and he released the woman and was taken into custody.

The MOST logical order for the above sentences to appear in the report is
A. I, III, II, IV, V   B. IV, III, II, I, V   C. III, II, I, IV, V   D. V, I, II, III, IV

8. Police Officer Byrnes is preparing a crime report concerning a robbery. The report will consist of the following five sentences:
   I. Mr. White, following the man's instructions, opened the car's hood, at which time the man got out of the auto, drew a revolver, and ordered White to give him all the money in his pockets.
   II. Investigation has determined there were no witnesses to this incident.
   III. The man asked White to check the oil and fill the tank.
   IV. Mr. White, a gas attendant, states that he was working alone at the gas station when a black male pulled up to the gas pump in a white Mercury.
   V. White was then bound and gagged by the male and locked in the gas station's rest room.

   The MOST logical order for the above sentences to appear in the report is
   A. IV, I, III, II, V   B. III, I, II, V, IV   C. IV, III, I, V, II   D. I, III, IV, II, V

9. Police Officer Gale is preparing a report of a crime committed against Mr. Weston. The report will consist of the following five sentences:
   I. The man, who had a gun, told Mr. Weston not to scream for help and ordered him back into the apartment.
   II. With Mr. Weston disposed of in this fashion, the man proceeded to ransack the apartment.
   III. Opening the door to see who was there, Mr. Weston was confronted by a tall white male wearing a dark blue jacket and white pants.
   IV. Mr. Weston was at home alone in his living room when the doorbell rang.
   V. Once inside, the man bound and gagged Mr. Weston and locked him in the bathroom.

   The MOST logical order for the above sentences to appear in the report is
   A. III, V, II, I, IV   B. IV, III, I, V, II   C. III, V, IV, II, I   D. IV, III, V, I, II

10. A police officer is completing a report of a robbery, which will contain the following five sentences:
    I. Two police officers were about to enter the Red Rose Coffee Shop on 47th Street and 8th Avenue.
    II. They then noticed a male running up the street carrying a brown paper bag.
    III. They heard a woman standing outside the Broadway Boutique yelling that her store had just been robbed by a young man, and she was pointing up the street.
    IV. They caught up with him and made an arrest.
    V. The police officers pursued the male, who ran past them on 8th Avenue.

    The MOST logical order for the above sentences to appear in the report is
    A. I, III, II, V, IV   B. III, I, II, V, IV   C. IV, V, I, II, III   D. I, V, IV, III, II

11. Police Officer Capalbo is preparing a report of a bank robbery. The report will contain the following five statements made by a witness:
    I. Initialing, all I could see were two men, dressed in maintenance uniforms, sitting in the area reserved for bank officers.
    II. I was passing the bank at 8 P.M. and noticed that all the lights were out, except in the rear section.
    III. Then I noticed two other men in the bank, coming from the direction of the vault, carrying a large metal box.
    IV. At this point, I decided to call the police.
    V. I knocked on the window to get the attention of the men in the maintenance uniforms, and they chased the two men carrying the box down a flight of steps.

    The MOST logical order for the above sentences to appear in the report is
       A. IV, I, II, V, III   B. I, III, II, V, IV   C. II, I, III, V, IV   D. II, III, I, V, IV

12. Police Officer Roberts is preparing a crime report concerning an assault and a stolen car. The report will contain the following five sentences:
    I. Upon leaving the store to return to his car, Winters noticed that a male unknown to him was sitting in his car.
    II. The man then re-entered Winters' car and drove away, fleeing north on 2nd Avenue.
    III. Mr. Winters stated that he parked his car in front of 235 East 25th Street and left the engine running while he went into the butcher shop at that location.
    IV. Mr. Robert Gering, a witness, stated that the male is known in the neighborhood as Bobby Rae and is believed to reside at 323 East 114th Street.
    V. When Winters approached the car and ordered the man to get out, the man got out of the auto and struck Winters with his fists, knocking him to the ground.

    The MOST logical order for the above sentences to appear in the report is
       A. III, II, V, I, IV   B. III, I, V, II, IV   C. I, IV, V, II, III   D. III, II, I, V, IV

13. Police Officer Robinson is preparing a crime report concerning the robbery of Mr. Edwards' store. The report will consist of the following five sentences:
    I. When the last customer left the store, the two men drew revolvers and ordered Mr. Edwards to give them all the money in the cash register.
    II. The men proceeded to the back of the store as if they were going to do some shopping.
    III. Janet Morley, a neighborhood resident, later reported that she saw the men enter a green Ford station wagon and flee northbound on Albany Avenue.
    IV. Edwards complied after which the gunmen ran from the store.
    V. Mr. Edwards states that he was stocking merchandise behind the store counter when two white males entered the store.

    The MOST logical order for the above sentences to appear in the report is
       A. V, II, III, I, IV   B. V, II, I, IV, III   C. II, I, V, IV, III   D. III, V, II, I, IV

14. Police Officer Wendell is preparing an accident report for a 6-car accident that occurred at the intersection of Bath Avenue and Bay Parkway. The report will consist of the following five sentences:
    I. A 2016 Volkswagen Beetle, traveling east on Bath Avenue, swerved to the left to avoid the Impala, and struck a 2014 Ford station wagon which was traveling west on Bath Avenue.
    II. The Seville then mounted the curb on the northeast corner of Bath Avenue and Bay Parkway and struck a light pole.
    III. A 2013 Buick Lesabre, traveling northbound on Bay Parkway directly behind the Impala, struck the Impala, pushing it into the intersection of Bath Avenue and Bay Parkway.
    IV. A 2015 Chevy Impala, traveling northbound on Bay Parkway, had stopped for a red light at Bath Avenue.
    V. A 2017 Toyota, traveling westbound on Bath Avenue, swerved to the right to avoid hitting the Ford station wagon, and struck a 2017 Cadillac Seville double-parked near the corner.
    The MOST logical order for the above sentences to appear in the report is
    A. IV, III, V, II, I   B. III, IV, V, II, I   C. IV, III, I, V, II   D. III, IV, V, I, II

15. The following five sentences are part of an Activity Log entry Police Officer Rogers made regarding an explosion:
    I. I quickly treated the pedestrian for the injury.
    II. The explosion caused a glass window in an office building to shatter.
    III. After the pedestrian was treated, a call was placed to the precinct requesting additional police officers to evacuate the area.
    IV. After all the glass settled to the ground, I saw a pedestrian who was bleeding from the arm.
    V. While on foot patrol near 5th Avenue and 53rd Street, I heard a loud explosion.
    The MOST logical order for the above sentences to appear in the report is
    A. II, V, IV, I, III   B. V, II, IV, III, I   C. V, II, I, IV, III   D. V, II, IV, I, III

16. Police Officer David is completing a report regarding illegal activity near the entrance to Madison Square Garden during a recent rock concert. The report will obtain the following five sentences:
    I. As I came closer to the man, he placed what appeared to be tickets in his pocket and began to walk away.
    II. After the man stopped, I questioned him about *scalping* tickets.
    III. While on assignment near the Madison Square Garden entrance, I observed a man apparently selling tickets.
    IV. I stopped the man by stating that I was a police officer.
    V. The man was then given a summons, and he left the area.
    The MOST logical order for the above sentences to appear in the report is
    A. I, III, IV, II, V   B. III, I, IV, V, II   C. III, IV, I, II, V   D. III, I, IV, II, V

17. Police Officer Sampson is preparing a report containing a dispute in a bar. The report will contain the following five sentences:
    I. John Evans, the bartender, ordered the two men out of the bar.
    II. Two men dressed in dungarees entered the C and D Bar at 5:30 P.M.
    III. The two men refused to leave and began to beat up Evans.
    IV. A customer in the bar saw me on patrol and yelled to me to come separate the three men.
    V. The two men became very drunk and loud within a short time.
    The MOST logical order for the above sentences to appear in the report is
       A. II, I, V, III, IV   B. II, III, IV, V, I   C. III, I, II, V, IV   D. II, V, I, III, IV

17.____

18. A police officer is completing a report concerning the response to a crime in progress. The report will include the following five sentences:
    I. The officers saw two armed men run out of the liquor store and into a waiting car.
    II. Police Officers Lunty and Duren received the call and responded to the liquor store.
    III. The robbers gave up without a struggle.
    IV. Lunty and Duren blocked the getaway car with their patrol car.
    V. A call came into the precinct concerning a robbery in progress at Jane's Liquor Store.
    The MOST logical order for the above sentence to appear in the report is
       A. V, II, I, IV, III   B. II, V, I, III, IV   C. V, I, IV, II, III   D. I, V, II, III, IV

18.____

19. Police Officers Jenkins is preparing a Crime Report which will consist of the following five sentences:
    I. After making inquirie in the vicinity, Smith found out that his next door neighbor, Viola Jones, had seen two local teenagers, Michael Heinz and Vincent Gaynor, smash his car's windshields with a crowbar.
    II. Jones told Smith that the teenagers live at 8700 19th Avenue.
    III. Mr. Smith heard a loud crash at approximately 11:00 P.M., looked out of his apartment window, and saw two white males running away from his car.
    IV. Smith then reported the incident to the precinct, and Heinz and Gaynor were arrested at the address given.
    V. Leaving his apartment to investigate further, Smith discovered that his car's front and rear windshields had been smashed.
    The MOST logical order for the above sentences to appear in the report is
       A. III, IV, V, I, II   B. III, V, I, II, IV   C. III, I, V, II, IV   D. V, III, I, II, IV

19.____

20. Sergeant Nancy Winston is reviewing a Gun Control Report which will contain the following five sentences:
    I. The man fell to the floor when hit in the chest with three bullets from 22 caliber gun.
    II. Merriam's 22 caliber gun was seized, and he was given a summons for not having a pistol permit.
    III. Christopher Merriam, the owner of A-Z Grocery, shot a man who attempted to rob him.
    IV. Police Officer Franks responded and asked Merriam for his pistol permit, which he could not produce.

20.____

V. Merriam phoned the police to report he had just shot a man who had attempted to rob him.

The MOST logical order for the above sentences to appear in the report is
A. III, I, V, IV, II B. I, III, V, IV, II C. III, I, V, II, IV D. I, III, II, V, IV

21. Detective John Manville is completing a report for his superior regarding the murder of an unknown male who was shot in Central Park. The report will contain the following five sentences:
    I. Police Officers Langston and Cavers responded to the scene.
    II. I received the assignment to investigate the murder in Central Park from Detective Sergeant Rogers.
    III. Langston notified the Detective Bureau after questioning Jason.
    IV. An unknown male, apparently murdered, was discovered in Central Park by Howard Jason, a park employee, who immediately called the police.
    V. Langston and Cavers questioned Jason.

    The MOST logical order for the above sentences to appear in the report is
    A. I, IV, V, III, II B. IV, I, V, II, III C. IV, I, V, III, II D. IV, V, I, III, II

21.____

22. A police officer is completing a report concerning the arrest of a juvenile. The report will contain the following five sentences:
    I. Sanders then telephoned Jay's parents from the precinct to inform them of their son's arrest.
    II. The store owner resisted, and Jay then shot him and ran from the store.
    III. Jay was transported directly to the precinct by Officer Sanders.
    IV. James Jay, a juvenile, walked into a candy store and announced a hold-up.
    V. Police Officer Sanders, while on patrol, arrested Jay a block from the candy store.

    The MOST logical order for the above sentences to appear in the report is
    A. IV, V, II, I, III B. IV, II, V, III, I C. II, IV, V, III, I D. V, IV, II, I, III

22.____

23. Police Officer Olsen prepared a crime report for a robbery which contained the following five sentences:
    I. Mr. Gordon was approached by this individual who then produced a gun and demanded the money from the cash register.
    II. The man then fled from the scene on foot, southbound on 5th Avenue.
    III. Mr. Gordon was working at the deli counter when a white male, 5'6", 150-160 lbs., wearing a green jacket and blue pants, entered the store.
    IV. Mr. Gordon complied with the man's demands and handed him the daily receipts.
    V. Further investigation has determined there are no other witnesses to this robbery.

    The MOST logical order for the above sentences to appear in the report is
    A. I, III, IV, V, II B. I, IV, II, III, V C. III, IV, I, V, II D. III, I, IV, II, V

23.____

24. Police Officer Bryant responded to 285 E. 31st Street to take a crime report of a burglary of Mr. Bond's home. The report will contain a brief description of the incident, consisting of the following five sentences:
    I. When Mr. Bond attempted to stop the burglar by grabbing him, he was pushed to the floor.
    II. The burglar had apparently gained access to the home by forcing open the 2nd floor bedroom window facing the fire escape.
    III. Mr. Bond sustained a head injury in the scuffle, and the burglar exited the home through the front door.
    IV. Finding nothing in the dresser, the burglar proceeded downstairs to the first floor, where he was confronted by Mr. Bond who was reading in the dining room.
    V. Once inside, he searched the drawers of the bedroom dresser.
    The MOST logical order for the above sentences to appear in the report is
       A. V, IV, I, II, III   B. II, V, IV, I, III   C. II, IV, V, III, I   D. III, II, I, V, IV

25. Police Officer Derringer responded to a call of a rape-homicide case in his patrol area and was ordered to prepare an incident report, which will contain the following five sentences:
    I. He pushed Miss Scott to the ground and forcibly raped her.
    II. Mary Scott was approached from behind by a white male, 5'7", 150-160 lbs. wearing dark pants and a white jacket.
    III. As Robinson approached the male, he ordered him to stop.
    IV. Screaming for help, Miss Scott alerted one John Robinson, a local grocer, who chased her assailant as he fled the scene.
    V. The male turned and fired two shots at Robinson, who fell to the ground mortally wounded.
    The MOST logical order for the above sentences to appear in the report is
       A. IV, III, I, II, V   B. II, IV, III, V, I   C. II, IV, I, V, III   D. II, I, IV, III, V

KEY (CORRECT ANSWERS)

1.	B	11.	C
2.	C	12.	B
3.	C	13.	B
4.	A	14.	C
5.	B	15.	D
6.	A	16.	D
7.	B	17.	D
8.	C	18.	A
9.	B	19.	B
10.	A	20.	A

21.	C
22.	B
23.	D
24.	B
25.	D

PREPARING WRITTEN MATERIALS

EXAMINATION SECTION
TEST 1

DIRECTIONS: Each question or incomplete statement is followed by several suggested answers or completions. Select the one that BEST answers the question or completes the statement. *PRINT THE LETTER OF THE CORRECT ANSWER IN THE SPACE AT THE RIGHT.*

Questions 1-25.

DIRECTIONS: Questions 1 through 25 consist of sentences which may or may not be examples of good English usage. Consider grammar, punctuation, spelling, capitalization, awkwardness, etc. Examine each sentence, and then choose the correct statement about it from the four choices below it. If the English usage in the sentence given is better than it would be with any of the changes suggested in options B, C, and D, choose option A. Do not choose an option that will change the meaning of the sentence.

1. According to Judge Frank, the grocer's sons found guilty of assault and sentenced last Thursday.

    A. This is an example of acceptable writing.
    B. A comma should be placed after the word *sentenced*.
    C. The word *were* should be placed after *sons*.
    D. The apostrophe in grocer's should be placed after the *s*.

2. The department heads assistant said that the stenographers should type duplicate copies of all contracts, leases, and bills.

    A. This is an example of acceptable writing.
    B. A comma should be placed before the word *contracts*.
    C. An apostrophe should be placed before the *s* in *heads*.
    D. Quotation marks should be placed before *the stenographers* and after *bills*.

3. The lawyers questioned the men to determine who was the true property owner?

    A. This is an example of acceptable writing.
    B. The phrase *questioned the men* should be changed to *asked the men questions*.
    C. The word *was* should be changed to *were*.
    D. The question mark should be changed to a period.

4. The terms stated in the present contract are more specific than those stated in the previous contract.

    A. This is an example of acceptable writing.
    B. The word *are* should be changed to *is*.
    C. The word *than* should be changed to *then*.
    D. The word *specific* should be changed to *specified*.

119

5. Of the few lawyers considered, the one who argued more skillful was chosen for the job. 5.____

   A. This is an example of acceptable writing.
   B. The word *more* should be replaced by the word *most*.
   C. The word *skillful* should be replaced by the word *skillfully*.
   D. The word *chosen* should be replaced by the word *selected*.

6. Each of the states has a court of appeals; some states have circuit courts. 6.____

   A. This is an example of acceptable writing.
   B. The semi-colon should be changed to a comma.
   C. The word *has* should be changed to *have*.
   D. The word *some* should be capitalized.

7. The court trial has greatly effected the child's mental condition. 7.____

   A. This is an example of acceptable writing.
   B. The word *effected* should be changed to *affected*.
   C. The word *greatly* should be placed after *effected*.
   D. The apostrophe in *child's* should be placed after the *s*.

8. Last week, the petition signed by all the officers was sent to the Better Business Bureau. 8.____

   A. This is an example of acceptable writing.
   B. The phrase *last week* should be placed after *officers*.
   C. A comma should be placed after *petition*.
   D. The word *was* should be changed to *were*.

9. Mr. Farrell claims that he requested form A-12, and three booklets describing court procedures. 9.____

   A. This is an example of acceptable writing.
   B. The word *that* should be eliminated.
   C. A colon should be placed after *requested*.
   D. The comma after *A-12* should be eliminated.

10. We attended a staff conference on Wednesday the new safety and fire rules were discussed. 10.____

    A. This is an example of acceptable writing.
    B. The words *safety, fire,* and *rules* should begin with capital letters.
    C. There should be a comma after the word *Wednesday*.
    D. There should be a period after the word *Wednesday,* and the word *the* should begin with a capital letter.

11. Neither the dictionary or the telephone directory could be found in the office library. 11.____

    A. This is an example of acceptable writing.
    B. The word *or* should be changed to *nor*.
    C. The word *library* should be spelled *libery*.
    D. The word *neither* should be changed to *either*.

12. The report would have been typed correctly if the typist could read the draft. 12.____

    A. This is an example of acceptable writing.
    B. The word *would* should be removed.
    C. The word *have* should be inserted after the word *could*.
    D. The word *correctly* should be changed to *correct*.

13. The supervisor brought the reports and forms to an employees desk. 13.____

    A. This is an example of acceptable writing.
    B. The word *brought* should be changed to *took*.
    C. There should be a comma after the word *reports* and a comma after the word *forms*.
    D. The word *employees* should be spelled *employee's*.

14. It's important for all the office personnel to submit their vacation schedules on time. 14.____

    A. This is an example of acceptable writing.
    B. The word *It's* should be spelled *Its*.
    C. The word *their* should be spelled *they're*.
    D. The word *personnel* should be spelled *personal*.

15. The supervisor wants that all staff members report to the office at 9:00 A.M. 15.____

    A. This is an example of acceptable writing.
    B. The word *that* should be removed and the word *to* should be inserted after the word *members*.
    C. There should be a comma after the word *wants* and a comma after the word *office*.
    D. The word *wants* should be changed to *want*, and the word *shall* should be inserted after the word *members*.

16. Every morning the clerk opens the office mail and distributes it. 16.____

    A. This is an example of acceptable writing.
    B. The word *opens* should be changed to *open*.
    C. The word *mail* should be changed to *letters*.
    D. The word *it* should be changed to *them*.

17. The secretary typed more fast on a desktop computer than on a tablet. 17.____

    A. This is an example of acceptable writing.
    B. The words *more fast* should be changed to *faster*.
    C. There should be a comma after the words *desktop computer*.
    D. The word *than* should be changed to *then*.

18. The typist used an extention cord in order to connect her typewriter to the outlet nearest to her desk. 18.____

    A. This is an example of acceptable writing.
    B. A period should be placed after the word *cord*, and the word *in* should have a capital *I*.
    C. A comma should be placed after the word *typewriter*.
    D. The word *extention* should be spelled *extension*.

19. He would have went to the conference if he had received an invitation.

    A. This is an example of acceptable writing.
    B. The word *went* should be replaced by the word *gone*.
    C. The word *had* should be replaced by *would have*.
    D. The word *conference* should be spelled *conferance*.

20. In order to make the report neater, he spent many hours rewriting it.

    A. This is an example of acceptable writing.
    B. The word *more* should be inserted before the word *neater*.
    C. There should be a colon after the word *neater*.
    D. The word *spent* should be changed to *have spent*.

21. His supervisor told him that he should of read the memorandum more carefully.

    A. This is an example of acceptable writing.
    B. The word *memorandum* should be spelled *memorandom*.
    C. The word *of* should be replaced by the word *have*.
    D. The word *carefully* should be replaced by the word *careful*.

22. It was decided that two separate reports should be written.

    A. This is an example of acceptable writing.
    B. A comma should be inserted after the word *decided*.
    C. The word *be* should be replaced by the word *been*.
    D. A colon should be inserted after the word *that*.

23. She don't seem to understand that the work must be done as soon as possible.

    A. This is an example of acceptable writing.
    B. The word *doesn't* should replace the word *don't*.
    C. The word *why* should replace the word *that*.
    D. The word *as* before the word *soon* should be eliminated.

24. He excepted praise from his supervisor for a job well done.

    A. This is an example of acceptable writing.
    B. The word *excepted* should be spelled *accepted*.
    C. The order of the words *well done* should be changed to *done well*.
    D. There should be a comma after the word *supervisor*.

25. What appears to be intentional errors in grammar occur several times in the passage.

    A. This is an example of acceptable writing.
    B. The word *occur* should be spelled *occurr*.
    C. The word *appears* should be changed to *appear*.
    D. The phrase *several times* should be changed to *from time to time*.

KEY (CORRECT ANSWERS)

1. C
2. C
3. D
4. A
5. C

6. A
7. B
8. A
9. D
10. D

11. B
12. C
13. D
14. A
15. B

16. A
17. B
18. D
19. B
20. A

21. C
22. A
23. B
24. B
25. C

TEST 2

DIRECTIONS: Each question consists of a sentence which may or may not be an example of good formal English usage. Examine each sentence, considering grammar, punctuation, spelling, capitalization, and awkwardness. Then choose the CORRECT statement about it from the four options below it. If the English usage in the sentence given is better than any of the changes suggested in options B, C, or D, pick option A. Do not pick an option that will change the meaning of the sentence. *PRINT THE LETTER OF THE CORRECT ANSWER IN THE SPACE AT THE RIGHT.*

1. I don't know who could possibly of broken it.   1.____

   A. This is an example of acceptable writing.
   B. The word *who* should be replaced by the word *whom*.
   C. The word *of* should be replaced by the word *have*.
   D. The word *broken* should be replaced by the word *broke*.

2. Telephoning is easier than to write.   2.____

   A. This is an example of acceptable writing.
   B. The word *telephoning* should be spelled *telephoneing*.
   C. The word *than* should be replaced by the word *then*.
   D. The words *to write* should be replaced by the word *writing*.

3. The two operators who have been assigned to these consoles are on vacation.   3.____

   A. This is an example of acceptable writing.
   B. A comma should be placed after the word *operators*.
   C. The word *who* should be replaced by the word *whom*.
   D. The word *are* should be replaced by the word *is*.

4. You were suppose to teach me how to operate a plugboard.   4.____

   A. This is an example of acceptable writing.
   B. The word *were* should be replaced by the word *was*.
   C. The word *suppose* should be replaced by the word *supposed*.
   D. The word *teach* should be replaced by the word *learn*.

5. If you had taken my advice; you would have spoken with him.   5.____

   A. This is an example of acceptable writing.
   B. The word *advice* should be spelled *advise*.
   C. The words *had taken* should be replaced by the word *take*.
   D. The semicolon should be changed to a comma.

6. The clerk could have completed the assignment on time if he knows where these materials were located.   6.____

   A. This is an example of acceptable writing.
   B. The word *knows* should be replaced by *had known*.
   C. The word *were* should be replaced by *had been*.
   D. The words *where these materials were located* should be replaced by *the location of these materials*.

124

7. All employees should be given safety training. Not just those who have accidents.   7._____

    A. This is an example of acceptable writing.
    B. The period after the word *training* should be changed to a colon.
    C. The period after the word *training* should be changed to a semicolon, and the first letter of the word *Not* should be changed to a small *n*.
    D. The period after the word *training* should be changed to a comma, and the first letter of the word *Not* should be changed to a small *n*.

8. This proposal is designed to promote employee awareness of the suggestion program, to encourage employee participation in the program, and to increase the number of suggestions submitted.   8._____

    A. This is an example of acceptable writing.
    B. The word *proposal* should be spelled *preposal*.
    C. The words *to increase the number of suggestions submitted* should be changed to *an increase in the number of suggestions is expected*.
    D. The word *promote* should be changed to *enhance,* and the word *increase* should be changed to *add to*.

9. The introduction of inovative managerial techniques should be preceded by careful analysis of the specific circumstances and conditions in each department.   9._____

    A. This is an example of acceptable writing.
    B. The word *techniques* should be spelled *techneques*.
    C. The word *inovative* should be spelled *innovative*.
    D. A comma should be placed after the word *circumstances* and after the word *conditions*.

10. This occurrence indicates that such criticism embarrasses him.   10._____

    A. This is an example of acceptable writing.
    B. The word *occurrence* should be spelled *occurence*.
    C. The word *criticism* should be spelled *criticism*.
    D. The word *embarrasses* should be spelled *embarasses*.

11. He can recommend a mechanic whose work is reliable.   11._____

    A. This is an example of acceptable writing.
    B. The word *reliable* should be spelled *relyable*.
    C. The word *whose* should be spelled *who's*.
    D. The word *mechanic* should be spelled *mecanic*.

12. She typed quickly; like someone who had not a moment to lose.   12._____

    A. This is an example of acceptable writing.
    B. The word *not* should be removed.
    C. The semicolon should be changed to a comma.
    D. The word *quickly* should be placed before instead of after the word *typed*.

13. She insisted that she had to much work to do.   13._____

    A. This is an example of acceptable writing.
    B. The word *insisted* should be spelled *insisted*.

C. The word *to* used in front of *much* should be spelled *too*.
D. The word *do* should be changed to *be done*.

14. The report, along with the accompanying documents, were submitted for review.   14.____

    A. This is an example of acceptable writing.
    B. The words *were submitted* should be changed to *was submitted*.
    C. The word *accompanying* should be spelled *accompaning*.
    D. The comma after the word *report* should be taken out.

15. If others must use your files, be certain that they understand how the system works, but insist that you do all the filing and refiling.   15.____

    A. This is an example of acceptable writing.
    B. There should be a period after the word *works,* and the word *but* should start a new sentence.
    C. The words *filing* and *refiling* should be spelled *fileing* and *refileing*.
    D. There should be a comma after the word *but*.

16. The appeal was not considered because of its late arrival.   16.____

    A. This is an example of acceptable writing.
    B. The word *its* should be changed to *it's*.
    C. The word *its* should be changed to *the*.
    D. The words *late arrival* should be changed to *arrival late*.

17. The letter must be read carefuly to determine under which subject it should be filed.   17.____

    A. This is an example of acceptable writing.
    B. The word *under* should be changed to *at*.
    C. The word *determine* should be spelled *determin*.
    D. The word *carefuly* should be spelled *carefully*.

18. He showed potential as an office manager, but he lacked skill in delegating work.   18.____

    A. This is an example of acceptable writing.
    B. The word *delegating* should be spelled *delagating*.
    C. The word *potential* should be spelled *potencial*.
    D. The words *he lacked* should be changed to *was lacking*.

19. His supervisor told him that it would be all right to receive personal mail at the office.   19.____

    A. This is an example of acceptable writing.
    B. The words *all right* should be changed to *alright*.
    C. The word *personal* should be spelled *personel*.
    D. The word *mail* should be changed to *letters*.

20. The report, along with the accompanying documents, were submitted for review.   20.____

    A. This is an example of acceptable writing.
    B. The words *were submitted* should be changed to *was submitted*.
    C. The word *accompanying* should be spelled *accompaning*.
    D. The comma after the word *report* should be taken out.

KEY (CORRECT ANSWERS)

1.	C	11.	A
2.	D	12.	C
3.	A	13.	C
4.	C	14.	B
5.	D	15.	A
6.	B	16.	A
7.	D	17.	D
8.	A	18.	A
9.	C	19.	A
10.	A	20.	B

PROCESS SERVER

PERTINENT EXCERPTS FROM THE CIVIL PRACTICE LAW AND RULES (CPLR)

§ 304. Method of commencing action or special proceeding

An action is commenced and jurisdiction acquired by service of a summons. A special proceeding is commenced and jurisdiction acquired by service of a notice of petition or orders to show cause.

Rule 305. Summons; supplemental summons, amendment

(a) **Summons; supplemental summons.** A summons shall specify the basis of the venue designated and if based upon the residence of the plaintiff it shall specify his address. The summons in an action arising out of a consumer credit transaction shall prominently display at the top' of the summons the words "consumer credit transaction" and, where a purchaser, borrower or debtor is a defendant, shall specify the county of residence of a defendant, if one resides within the state, and the county where the consumer credit transaction took place, if it is within the. state. Where the court directs that a new party be joined in the action and the order is not made upon the new party's motion, a supplemental summons specifying the pleading which he must answer shall be served upon him.

(b) **Summons and notice.** If the complaint is not served with the summons, the summons may contain or have attached thereto a notice stating the object of the action and the relief sought, and, in an action for a sum certain or for a sum which can by computation be made certain, the sum of money for which judgment will be taken in case of default.

(c) **Amendment.** At any time, in its discretion and upon such terms as it deems just, the court may allow any summons or proof of service of a summons to be amended, if a substantial right of a party against whom the summons issued is not prejudiced.

§ 306. Proof of service

(a) **Generally.** Proof of service shall specify the papers served, the person who was served and the date, time, address, or, in the event there is no address, place and manner of service, and set forth facts showing that the service was made by an authorized person and in an authorized manner.

(b) **Personal service.** Whenever service is made pursuant to this article by delivery of the summons to an individual, proof of service shall also include, in addition to any other requirement, a description of the person to whom it was so delivered, including, but not limited to, sex, color of skin, hair color. approximate age, approximate weight and height, and other identifying features.

(c) **Other service.** Where service is made pursuant to subdivision four of section three hundred, eight of this chapter, proof of service shall also specify the dates, addresses and the times of attempted service pursuant to subdivisions one, two or three of such section.

(d) **Form.** Proof of service shall be in the form of a certificate if the service is made by a sheriff or other authorized public officer or in the form of an affidavit if made by any other person.

(e) **Admission of service.** A writing admitting service by the person to be served is adequate proof of service.

§ 307. Personal service upon the state

Personal service upon the state shall be made by delivering the summons to an assistant attorney general at an office of the attorney general or to the attorney general within the state.

§ 308. Personal service upon a natural person·

Personal service upon a natural person shall be made by any of the following methods:

1. by delivering the summons within the state to the person to be served; or

2. by delivering the summons within the state to a person of suitable age and discretion at the actual place of business, dwelling place or usual place of abode of the person to be served and by mailing the summons to the person to be served at his last known residence; proof of such service shall be filed within twenty days thereafter with the clerk of the court designated in the summons; service shall be complete ten days after such filing; proof of service shall identify such person of suitable age and discretion and state the date, time and place of service, except in matrimonial actions where service hereunder may be made pursuant to an order made in accordance with the provisions of subdivision a of section two hundred thirty-two of the domestic relations law; or

3. by delivering the summons within the state to the agent for service of the person to be served as designated under rule 318, except in matrimonial actions where service hereunder may be made pursuant to an order made in accordance with the provisions of subdivision a of section two hundred thirty-two of the domestic relations law;

4. where service under paragraphs one and two cannot be made with due diligence, by affixing the summons to the door of either the actual place of business,. dwelling place or usual place of abode within the state of the person to be served and by mailing the summons to such person at his last known residence; proof of such service shall be filed within twenty days thereafter with the clerk of the court designated in the summons; service shall be complete ten days after such filing, except in matrimonial actions where service hereunder may be made pursuant to an order made in accordance with the provisions of subdivision a of section two hundred thirty-two of the domestic relations law;

5. in such manner as the court, upon motion without notice, directs, if service is impracticable under paragraphs one, two and four of this section.

Notwithstanding any other provision of law in an action against a natural person based upon nonpayment of any contractual obligation additional notice must be given by the plaintiff or the attorney for the plaintiff, at least twenty days prior to entry of any default judgment, by mailing a copy of the summons by first class mail to the defendant at his last known residence address; or in the event such mailing is returned as undeliverable by the post office prior to the entry of a default judgment, or if the residence address of the defendant is unknown, then to the defendant in care of the place of employment of the defendant if known, in an envelope bearing the legend "personal and confidential" and not indicating on the outside thereof, by the return address or otherwise, that the communication is from an attorney or concerns an alleged debt; or if neither the residence address nor the place of employment of the defendant is known, then to the defendant at any other known address. An affidavit of any mailing pursuant to this paragraph shall be executed by the person mailing the summons and filed with the judgment. Failure to comply with the requirements of this paragraph shall not be the basis of any relief in the event that the defendant enters an appearance in the action prior to judgment. The requirements of this paragraph shall not apply to cases in the small claims part or division of any court or in relation to summary proceedings to recover possession of real property.

§ 309. Personal service upon an infant or incompetent

(a) Upon an infant. Personal service upon an infant shall be made by personally serving the summons within the state upon a parent or any guardian or any person having legal custody or, if the infant is married, upon an adult spouse with whom the infant resides, or, if none are within the state, upon any other person with whom he resides, or by whom he is employed. If the infant is of the age of fourteen years or over, the summons shall also be personally served upon him within the state.

(b) Upon a person judicially declared to be incompetent. Personal service upon a person judicially declared to be incompetent to manage his affairs and for whom a committee has been appointed -Shall be made by personally serving the summons within the state upon the committee and upon the incompetent, but the court may dispense with service upon the incompetent.

§ 310. Personal" service upon a partnership

Personal service upon persons conducting a business as a partnership may be made by personally serving the summons within the state upon anyone of them.

§ 311. Personal service upon a corporation or governmental subdivision

Personal service upon a corporation or governmental subdivision shall be made by delivering the summons as follows:

1. upon any domestic or foreign corporation, to an officer, director, managing or general agent, or cashier or assistant cashier or to any other agent authorized by appointment or by law to receive service;

2. upon the city of New York, to the corporation counselor to any person designated by him to receive process in a writing filed in the office of the clerk of New York county;

3. upon any other city, to the mayor, comptroller, treasurer, counselor clerk; or, if the city lacks such officers, to an officer performing a corresponding function under another name)

4. upon a county, to the chairman or clerk of the board of supervisors, clerk, attorney or treasurer;
5. upon a town, to the supervisor or the clerk;
6. upon a village, to the mayor, clerk, or any trustee;

7. upon a school district, to a school officer, as defined in the education law; and

8. upon a park, sewage or other district, to the clerk, any trustee or any member of the board.

§ 312. Personal service upon a court, board or commission

'Personal service upon a court consisting of three or more judges may be, made by delivering the summons to anyone of them. Personal, service upon a board or commission having a chairman or other presiding officer, secretary or clerk, by whatever official title he is called, may be made by delivering the summons to" him. Personal service upon any other board or commission shall be made by delivering the summons to anyone of the members.

§ 313. Service without the state giving personal jurisdiction

A person domiciled in the state or subject to the jurisdiction of the courts of the state under section 301 or 302, or his executor or administrator, may be served with the summons without the state, in the same manner as service is made within the state, by any person authorized to make service within the state who is a resident of the state or by any person authorized to make service by the laws of the state, territory, possession or country in which service is made or by any duly qualified attorney, solicitor, barrister, or equivalent in such jurisdiction.

§ 314. Service without the state not giving personal jurisdiction in certain actions

Service may be made without the state by any person authorized by section 313 in the same manner as service is made within the state:

1. in a matrimonial action; or

2. where a judgment is demanded that the person to be served be excluded from a vested or contingent interest in or lien upon specific real or personal property within the state; or that such an interest or lien in favor of either party be enforced, regulated, defined or limited; or otherwise affecting the title to such property, including an action of interpleader or defensive interpleader; or

3. where a levy upon property of the person to be served has been made within the state pursuant to an order of attachment or a chattel of such person has been seized in an action to recover a chattel.

§ 315. Service by publication authorized

The court, upon motion without notice, shall order service of a summons by publication in an action described in section 314 if service cannot be made by another prescribed method with due diligence.

Rule 316. Service by publication

(a) Contents of order; form of publication; filing. An order for service of a summons by publication shall direct that the summons be published together with the notice to the defendant, a brief statement of the object of the action and, if the action is brought to recover a judgment affecting the title to, or the possession, use or enjoyment of, real property, a brief description of the property, in two newspapers, at least one in the English language, designated in the order as most likely to give notice to the person to be served, for a specified time, at least once in each of four successive weeks, except that in the matrimonial action publication in one newspaper in the English language, designated in the order as most likely to give notice to the person to be served, at least once in each of three successive weeks shall be sufficient. The summons, complaint, or summons and notice in an action for divorce or separation, order and papers on which the order was based shall be filed on or before the first day of publication.

(b) Mailing to accompany publication in matrimonial actions. An order for service of a summons by publication in a matrimonial action shall also direct that on or before the first day of publication a copy of the summons be mailed to the person to be served unless a place where such person probably would receive mail cannot with due diligence be ascertained and the court dispenses with such mailing. A notice of publication shall be enclosed.

(c) Time of publication; when service complete. The first publication of the summons shall be made within twenty days after the order is granted. Service by publication is complete on the twenty-eighth day after the day of first publication, except that in a matrimonial action it is complete on the twenty-first day after the day of first publication.

§ 317. Defense by person to whom summons not personally delivered

A person served with a summons other than by personal delivery to him or his agent for service designated under rule 318, within or without the state, who does not appear may be allowed to defend the action within one year after he obtains knowledge of entry of the judgment, but in no event more than five years after such entry, upon a finding of the court that he did not personally receive notice of the summons in time to defend and has a meritorious defense. If the defense is successful, the court may direct and enforce restitution in the same manner and subject to the

Rule 318. Designation of agent for service

A person may be designated- by a natural person, corporation or partnership as an agent for service in writing with the consent of the agent endorsed thereon. The writing shall be filed in the office of the clerk of the county in which the principal to be served resides or has its principal office. The, designation shall remain in effect for three years from such filing unless it has been revoked by the filing of a revocation, or by the death, judicial declaration of incompetency or legal termination of the agent or principal.

GLOSSARY OF LEGAL TERMS

TABLE OF CONTENTS

	Page
Action ... Affiant	1
Affidavit ... At Bar	2
At Issue ... Burden of Proof	3
Business ... Commute	4
Complainant ... Conviction	5
Cooperative ... Demur (v.)	6
Demurrage ... Endorsement	7
Enjoin ... Facsimile	8
Factor ... Guilty	9
Habeas Corpus ... Incumbrance	10
Indemnify ... Laches	11
Landlord and Tenant ... Malice	12
Mandamus ... Obiter Dictum	13
Object (v.) ... Perjury	14
Perpetuity ... Proclamation	15
Proffered Evidence ... Referee	16
Referendum ... Stare Decisis	17
State ... Term	18
Testamentary ... Warrant (Warranty) (v.)	19
Warrant (n.) ... Zoning	20

GLOSSARY OF LEGAL TERMS

A

ACTION - "Action" includes a civil action and a criminal action.
A FORTIORI - A term meaning you can reason one thing from the existence of certain facts.
A POSTERIORI - From what goes after; from effect to cause.
A PRIORI - From what goes before; from cause to effect.
AB INITIO - From the beginning.
ABATE - To diminish or put an end to.
ABET - To encourage the commission of a crime.
ABEYANCE - Suspension, temporary suppression.
ABIDE - To accept the consequences of.
ABJURE - To renounce; give up.
ABRIDGE - To reduce; contract; diminish.
ABROGATE - To annul, repeal, or destroy.
ABSCOND - To hide or absent oneself to avoid legal action.
ABSTRACT - A summary.
ABUT - To border on, to touch.
ACCESS - Approach; in real property law it means the right of the owner of property to the use of the highway or road next to his land, without obstruction by intervening property owners.
ACCESSORY - In criminal law, it means the person who contributes or aids in the commission of a crime.
ACCOMMODATED PARTY - One to whom credit is extended on the strength of another person signing a commercial paper.
ACCOMMODATION PAPER - A commercial paper to which the accommodating party has put his name.
ACCOMPLICE - In criminal law, it means a person who together with the principal offender commits a crime.
ACCORD - An agreement to accept something different or less than that to which one is entitled, which extinguishes the entire obligation.
ACCOUNT - A statement of mutual demands in the nature of debt and credit between parties.
ACCRETION - The act of adding to a thing; in real property law, it means gradual accumulation of land by natural causes.
ACCRUE - To grow to; to be added to.
ACKNOWLEDGMENT - The act of going before an official authorized to take acknowledgments, and acknowledging an act as one's own.
ACQUIESCENCE - A silent appearance of consent.
ACQUIT - To legally determine the innocence of one charged with a crime.
AD INFINITUM - Indefinitely.
AD LITEM - For the suit.
AD VALOREM - According to value.
ADJECTIVE LAW - Rules of procedure.
ADJUDICATION - The judgment given in a case.
ADMIRALTY - Court having jurisdiction over maritime cases.
ADULT - Sixteen years old or over (in criminal law).
ADVANCE - In commercial law, it means to pay money or render other value before it is due.
ADVERSE - Opposed; contrary.
ADVOCATE - (v.) To speak in favor of;
          (n.) One who assists, defends, or pleads for another.
AFFIANT - A person who makes and signs an affidavit.

AFFIDAVIT - A written and sworn to declaration of facts, voluntarily made.
AFFINITY- The relationship between persons through marriage with the kindred of each other; distinguished from consanguinity, which is the relationship by blood.
AFFIRM - To ratify; also when an appellate court affirms a judgment, decree, or order, it means that it is valid and right and must stand as rendered in the lower court.
AFOREMENTIONED; AFORESAID - Before or already said.
AGENT - One who represents and acts for another.
AID AND COMFORT - To help; encourage.
ALIAS - A name not one's true name.
ALIBI - A claim of not being present at a certain place at a certain time.
ALLEGE - To assert.
ALLOTMENT - A share or portion.
AMBIGUITY - Uncertainty; capable of being understood in more than one way.
AMENDMENT - Any language made or proposed as a change in some principal writing.
AMICUS CURIAE - A friend of the court; one who has an interest in a case, although not a party in the case, who volunteers advice upon matters of law to the judge. For example, a brief amicus curiae.
AMORTIZATION - To provide for a gradual extinction of (a future obligation) in advance of maturity, especially, by periodical contributions to a sinking fund which will be adequate to discharge a debt or make a replacement when it becomes necessary.
ANCILLARY - Aiding, auxiliary.
ANNOTATION - A note added by way of comment or explanation.
ANSWER - A written statement made by a defendant setting forth the grounds of his defense.
ANTE - Before.
ANTE MORTEM - Before death.
APPEAL - The removal of a case from a lower court to one of superior jurisdiction for the purpose of obtaining a review.
APPEARANCE - Coming into court as a party to a suit.
APPELLANT - The party who takes an appeal from one court or jurisdiction to another (appellate) court for review.
APPELLEE - The party against whom an appeal is taken.
APPROPRIATE - To make a thing one's own.
APPROPRIATION - Prescribing the destination of a thing; the act of the legislature designating a particular fund, to be applied to some object of government expenditure.
APPURTENANT - Belonging to; accessory or incident to.
ARBITER - One who decides a dispute; a referee.
ARBITRARY - Unreasoned; not governed by any fixed rules or standard.
ARGUENDO - By way of argument.
ARRAIGN - To call the prisoner before the court to answer to a charge.
ASSENT - A declaration of willingness to do something in compliance with a request.
ASSERT - Declare.
ASSESS - To fix the rate or amount.
ASSIGN - To transfer; to appoint; to select for a particular purpose.
ASSIGNEE - One who receives an assignment.
ASSIGNOR - One who makes an assignment.
AT BAR - Before the court.

AT ISSUE - When parties in an action come to a point where one asserts something and the other denies it.
ATTACH - Seize property by court order and sometimes arrest a person.
ATTEST - To witness a will, etc.; act of attestation.
AVERMENT - A positive statement of facts.

B

BAIL - To obtain the release of a person from legal custody by giving security and promising that he shall appear in court; to deliver (goods, etc.) in trust to a person for a special purpose.
BAILEE - One to whom personal property is delivered under a contract of bailment.
BAILMENT - Delivery of personal property to another to be held for a certain purpose and to be returned when the purpose is accomplished.
BAILOR - The party who delivers goods to another, under a contract of bailment.
BANC (OR BANK) - Bench; the place where a court sits permanently or regularly; also the assembly of all the judges of a court.
BANKRUPT - An insolvent person, technically, one declared to be bankupt after a bankruptcy proceeding.
BAR - The legal profession.
BARRATRY - Exciting groundless judicial proceedings.
BARTER - A contract by which parties exchange goods for other goods.
BATTERY - Illegal interfering with another's person.
BEARER - In commercial law, it means the person in possession of a commercial paper which is payable to the bearer.
BENCH - The court itself or the judge.
BENEFICIARY - A person benefiting under a will, trust, or agreement.
BEST EVIDENCE RULE, THE - Except as otherwise provided by statute, no evidence other than the writing itself is admissible to prove the content of a writing. This section shall be known and may be cited as the best evidence rule.
BEQUEST - A gift of personal property under a will.
BILL - A formal written statement of complaint to a court of justice; also, a draft of an act of the legislature before it becomes a law; also, accounts for goods sold, services rendered, or work done.
BONA FIDE - In or with good faith; honestly.
BOND - An instrument by which the maker promises to pay a sum of money to another, usually providing that upon performances of a certain condition the obligation shall be void.
BOYCOTT - A plan to prevent the carrying on of a business by wrongful means.
BREACH - The breaking or violating of a law, or the failure to carry out a duty.
BRIEF - A written document, prepared by a lawyer to serve as the basis of an argument upon a case in court, usually an appellate court.
BURDEN OF PRODUCING EVIDENCE - The obligation of a party to introduce evidence sufficient to avoid a ruling against him on the issue.
BURDEN OF PROOF - The obligation of a party to establish by evidence a requisite degree of belief concerning a fact in the mind of the trier of fact or the court. The burden of proof may require a party to raise a reasonable doubt concerning the existence of nonexistence of a fact or that he establish the existence or nonexistence of a fact by a preponderance of the evidence, by clear and convincing proof, or by proof beyond a reasonable doubt.

Except as otherwise provided by law, the burden of proof requires proof by a preponderance of the evidence.

BUSINESS, A - Shall include every kind of business, profession, occupation, calling or operation of institutions, whether carried on for profit or not.

BY-LAWS - Regulations, ordinances, or rules enacted by a corporation, association, etc., for its own government.

C

CANON - A doctrine; also, a law or rule, of a church or association in particular.

CAPIAS - An order to arrest.

CAPTION - In a pleading, deposition or other paper connected with a case in court, it is the heading or introductory clause which shows the names of the parties, name of the court, number of the case on the docket or calendar, etc.

CARRIER - A person or corporation undertaking to transport persons or property.

CASE - A general term for an action, cause, suit, or controversy before a judicial body.

CAUSE - A suit, litigation or action before a court.

CAVEAT EMPTOR - Let the buyer beware. This term expresses the rule that the purchaser of an article must examine, judge, and test it for himself, being bound to discover any obvious defects or imperfections.

CERTIFICATE - A written representation that some legal formality has been complied with.

CERTIORARI - To be informed of; the name of a writ issued by a superior court directing the lower court to send up to the former the record and proceedings of a case.

CHANGE OF VENUE - To remove place of trial from one place to another.

CHARGE - An obligation or duty; a formal complaint; an instruction of the court to the jury upon a case.

CHARTER - (n.) The authority by virtue of which an organized body acts;
   (v.) in mercantile law, it means to hire or lease a vehicle or vessel for transportation.

CHATTEL - An article of personal property.

CHATTEL MORTGAGE - A mortgage on personal property.

CIRCUIT - A division of the country, for the administration of justice; a geographical area served by a court.

CITATION - The act of the court by which a person is summoned or cited; also, a reference to legal authority.

CIVIL (ACTIONS)- It indicates the private rights and remedies of individuals in contrast to the word "criminal" (actions) which relates to prosecution for violation of laws.

CLAIM (n.) - Any demand held or asserted as of right.

CODICIL - An addition to a will.

CODIFY - To arrange the laws of a country into a code.

COGNIZANCE - Notice or knowledge.

COLLATERAL - By the side; accompanying; an article or thing given to secure performance of a promise.

COMITY - Courtesy; the practice by which one court follows the decision of another court on the same question.

COMMIT - To perform, as an act; to perpetrate, as a crime; to send a person to prison.

COMMON LAW - As distinguished from law created by the enactment of the legislature (called statutory law), it relates to those principles and rules of action which derive their authority solely from usages and customs of immemorial antiquity, particularly with reference to the ancient unwritten law of England. The written pronouncements of the common law are found in court decisions.

COMMUTE - Change punishment to one less severe.

COMPLAINANT - One who applies to the court for legal redress.
COMPLAINT - The pleading of a plaintiff in a civil action; or a charge that a person has committed a specified offense.
COMPROMISE - An arrangement for settling a dispute by agreement.
CONCUR - To agree, consent.
CONCURRENT - Running together, at the same time.
CONDEMNATION - Taking private property for public use on payment therefor.
CONDITION - Mode or state of being; a qualification or restriction.
CONDUCT - Active and passive behavior; both verbal and nonverbal.
CONFESSION - Voluntary statement of guilt of crime.
CONFIDENTIAL COMMUNICATION BETWEEN CLIENT AND LAWYER - Information transmitted between a client and his lawyer in the course of that relationship and in confidence by a means which, so far as the client is aware, discloses the information to no third persons other than those who are present to further the interest of the client in the consultation or those to whom disclosure is reasonably necessary for the transmission of the information or the accomplishment of the purpose for which the lawyer is consulted, and includes a legal opinion formed and the advice given by the lawyer in the course of that relationship.
CONFRONTATION - Witness testifying in presence of defendant.
CONSANGUINITY - Blood relationship.
CONSIGN - To give in charge; commit; entrust; to send or transmit goods to a merchant, factor, or agent for sale.
CONSIGNEE - One to whom a consignment is made.
CONSIGNOR - One who sends or makes a consignment.
CONSPIRACY - In criminal law, it means an agreement between two or more persons to commit an unlawful act.
CONSPIRATORS - Persons involved in a conspiracy.
CONSTITUTION - The fundamental law of a nation or state.
CONSTRUCTION OF GENDERS - The masculine gender includes the feminine and neuter.
CONSTRUCTION OF SINGULAR AND PLURAL - The singular number includes the plural; and the plural, the singular.
CONSTRUCTION OF TENSES - The present tense includes the past and future tenses; and the future, the present.
CONSTRUCTIVE - An act or condition assumed from other parts or conditions.
CONSTRUE - To ascertain the meaning of language.
CONSUMMATE - To complete.
CONTIGUOUS - Adjoining; touching; bounded by.
CONTINGENT - Possible, but not assured; dependent upon some condition.
CONTINUANCE - The adjournment or postponement of an action pending in a court.
CONTRA - Against, opposed to; contrary.
CONTRACT - An agreement between two or more persons to do or not to do a particular thing.
CONTROVERT - To dispute, deny.
CONVERSION - Dealing with the personal property of another as if it were one's own, without right.
CONVEYANCE - An instrument transferring title to land.
CONVICTION - Generally, the result of a criminal trial which ends in a judgment or sentence that the defendant is guilty as charged.

COOPERATIVE - A cooperative is a voluntary organization of persons with a common interest, formed and operated along democratic lines for the purpose of supplying services at cost to its members and other patrons, who contribute both capital and business.
CORPUS DELICTI - The body of a crime; the crime itself.
CORROBORATE - To strengthen; to add weight by additional evidence.
COUNTERCLAIM - A claim presented by a defendant in opposition to or deduction from the claim of the plaintiff.
COUNTY - Political subdivision of a state.
COVENANT - Agreement.
CREDIBLE - Worthy of belief.
CREDITOR - A person to whom a debt is owing by another person, called the "debtor."
CRIMINAL ACTION - Includes criminal proceedings.
CRIMINAL INFORMATION - Same as complaint.
CRITERION (sing.)
CRITERIA (plural) - A means or tests for judging; a standard or standards.
CROSS-EXAMINATION - Examination of a witness by a party other than the direct examiner upon a matter that is within the scope of the direct examination of the witness.
CULPABLE - Blamable.
CY-PRES - As near as (possible). The rule of *cy-pres* is a rule for the construction of instruments in equity by which the intention of the party is carried out *as near as may be*, when it would be impossible or illegal to give it literal effect.

D

DAMAGES - A monetary compensation, which may be recovered in the courts by any person who has suffered loss, or injury, whether to his person, property or rights through the unlawful act or omission or negligence of another.
DECLARANT - A person who makes a statement.
DE FACTO - In fact; actually but without legal authority.
DE JURE - Of right; legitimate; lawful.
DE MINIMIS - Very small or trifling.
DE NOVO - Anew; afresh; a second time.
DEBT - A specified sum of money owing to one person from another, including not only the obligation of the debtor to pay, but the right of the creditor to receive and enforce payment.
DECEDENT - A dead person.
DECISION - A judgment or decree pronounced by a court in determination of a case.
DECREE - An order of the court, determining the rights of all parties to a suit.
DEED - A writing containing a contract sealed and delivered; particularly to convey real property.
DEFALCATION - Misappropriation of funds.
DEFAMATION - Injuring one's reputation by false statements.
DEFAULT - The failure to fulfill a duty, observe a promise, discharge an obligation, or perform an agreement.
DEFENDANT - The person defending or denying; the party against whom relief or recovery is sought in an action or suit.
DEFRAUD - To practice fraud; to cheat or trick.
DELEGATE (v.)- To entrust to the care or management of another.
DELICTUS - A crime.
DEMUR (v.) - To dispute the sufficiency in law of the pleading of the other side.

DEMURRAGE - In maritime law, it means, the sum fixed or allowed as remuneration to the owners of a ship for the detention of their vessel beyond the number of days allowed for loading and unloading or for sailing; also used in railroad terminology.
DENIAL - A form of pleading; refusing to admit the truth of a statement, charge, etc.
DEPONENT - One who gives testimony under oath reduced to writing.
DEPOSITION - Testimony given under oath outside of court for use in court or for the purpose of obtaining information in preparation for trial of a case.
DETERIORATION - A degeneration such as from decay, corrosion or disintegration.
DETRIMENT - Any loss or harm to person or property.
DEVIATION - A turning aside.
DEVISE - A gift of real property by the last will and testament of the donor.
DICTUM (sing.)
DICTA (plural) - Any statements made by the court in an opinion concerning some rule of law not necessarily involved nor essential to the determination of the case.
DIRECT EVIDENCE - Evidence that directly proves a fact, without an inference or presumption, and which in itself if true, conclusively establishes that fact.
DIRECT EXAMINATION - The first examination of a witness upon a matter that is not within the scope of a previous examination of the witness.
DISAFFIRM - To repudiate.
DISMISS - In an action or suit, it means to dispose of the case without any further consideration or hearing.
DISSENT - To denote disagreement of one or more judges of a court with the decision passed by the majority upon a case before them.
DOCKET (n.) - A formal record, entered in brief, of the proceedings in a court.
DOCTRINE - A rule, principle, theory of law.
DOMICILE - That place where a man has his true, fixed and permanent home to which whenever he is absent he has the intention of returning.
DRAFT (n.) - A commercial paper ordering payment of money drawn by one person on another.
DRAWEE - The person who is requested to pay the money.
DRAWER - The person who draws the commercial paper and addresses it to the drawee.
DUPLICATE - A counterpart produced by the same impression as the original enlargements and miniatures, or by mechanical or electronic re-recording, or by chemical reproduction, or by other equivalent technique which accurately reproduces the original.
DURESS - Use of force to compel performance or non-performance of an act.

E

EASEMENT - A liberty, privilege, or advantage without profit, in the lands of another.
EGRESS - Act or right of going out or leaving; emergence.
EIUSDEM GENERIS - Of the same kind, class or nature. A rule used in the construction of language in a legal document.
EMBEZZLEMENT - To steal; to appropriate fraudulently to one's own use property entrusted to one's care.
EMBRACERY - Unlawful attempt to influence jurors, etc., but not by offering value.
EMINENT DOMAIN - The right of a state to take private property for public use.
ENACT - To make into a law.
ENDORSEMENT - Act of writing one's name on the back of a note, bill or similar written instrument.

ENJOIN - To require a person, by writ of injunction from a court of equity, to perform or to abstain or desist from some act.
ENTIRETY - The whole; that which the law considers as one whole, and not capable of being divided into parts.
ENTRAPMENT - Inducing one to commit a crime so as to arrest him.
ENUMERATED - Mentioned specifically; designated.
ENURE - To operate or take effect.
EQUITY - In its broadest sense, this term denotes the spirit and the habit of fairness, justness, and right dealing which regulate the conduct of men.
ERROR - A mistake of law, or the false or irregular application of law as will nullify the judicial proceedings.
ESCROW - A deed, bond or other written engagement, delivered to a third person, to be delivered by him only upon the performance or fulfillment of some condition.
ESTATE - The interest which any one has in lands, or in any other subject of property.
ESTOP - To stop, bar, or impede.
ESTOPPEL - A rule of law which prevents a man from alleging or denying a fact, because of his own previous act.
ET AL. (alii) - And others.
ET SEQ. (sequential) - And the following.
ET UX. (uxor) - And wife.
EVIDENCE - Testimony, writings, material objects, or other things presented to the senses that are offered to prove the existence or non-existence of a fact.
    Means from which inferences may be drawn as a basis of proof in duly constituted judicial or fact finding tribunals, and includes testimony in the form of opinion and hearsay.
EX CONTRACTU
EX DELICTO - In law, rights and causes of action are divided into two classes, those arising *ex contractu* (from a contract) and those arising *ex delicto* (from a delict or tort).
EX OFFICIO - From office; by virtue of the office.
EX PARTE - On one side only; by or for one.
EX POST FACTO - After the fact.
EX POST FACTO LAW - A law passed after an act was done which retroactively makes such act a crime.
EX REL. (relations) - Upon relation or information.
EXCEPTION - An objection upon a matter of law to a decision made, either before or after judgment by a court.
EXECUTOR (male)
EXECUTRIX (female) - A person who has been appointed by will to execute the will.
EXECUTORY - That which is yet to be executed or performed.
EXEMPT - To release from some liability to which others are subject.
EXONERATION - The removal of a burden, charge or duty.
EXTRADITION - Surrender of a fugitive from one nation to another.

F

F.A.S.- "Free alongside ship"; delivery at dock for ship named.
F.O.B.- "Free on board"; seller will deliver to car, truck, vessel, or other conveyance by which goods are to be transported, without expense or risk of loss to the buyer or consignee.
FABRICATE - To construct; to invent a false story.
FACSIMILE - An exact or accurate copy of an original instrument.

FACTOR - A commercial agent.
FEASANCE - The doing of an act.
FELONIOUS - Criminal, malicious.
FELONY - Generally, a criminal offense that may be punished by death or imprisonment for more than one year as differentiated from a misdemeanor.
FEME SOLE - A single woman.
FIDUCIARY - A person who is invested with rights and powers to be exercised for the benefit of another person.
FIERI FACIAS - A writ of execution commanding the sheriff to levy and collect the amount of a judgment from the goods and chattels of the judgment debtor.
FINDING OF FACT - Determination from proof or judicial notice of the existence of a fact. A ruling implies a supporting finding of fact; no separate or formal finding is required unless required by a statute of this state.
FISCAL - Relating to accounts or the management of revenue.
FORECLOSURE (sale) - A sale of mortgaged property to obtain satisfaction of the mortgage out of the sale proceeds.
FORFEITURE - A penalty, a fine.
FORGERY - Fabricating or producing falsely, counterfeited.
FORTUITOUS - Accidental.
FORUM - A court of justice; a place of jurisdiction.
FRAUD - Deception; trickery.
FREEHOLDER - One who owns real property.
FUNGIBLE - Of such kind or nature that one specimen or part may be used in the place of another.

G

GARNISHEE - Person garnished.
GARNISHMENT - A legal process to reach the money or effects of a defendant, in the possession or control of a third person.
GRAND JURY - Not less than 16, not more than 23 citizens of a county sworn to inquire into crimes committed or triable in the county.
GRANT - To agree to; convey, especially real property.
GRANTEE - The person to whom a grant is made.
GRANTOR - The person by whom a grant is made.
GRATUITOUS - Given without a return, compensation or consideration.
GRAVAMEN - The grievance complained of or the substantial cause of a criminal action.
GUARANTY (n.) - A promise to answer for the payment of some debt, or the performance of some duty, in case of the failure of another person, who, in the first instance, is liable for such payment or performance.
GUARDIAN - The person, committee, or other representative authorized by law to protect the person or estate or both of an incompetent (or of a *sui juris* person having a guardian) and to act for him in matters affecting his person or property or both. An incompetent is a person under disability imposed by law.
GUILTY - Establishment of the fact that one has committed a breach of conduct; especially, a violation of law.

H

HABEAS CORPUS - You have the body; the name given to a variety of writs, having for their object to bring a party before a court or judge for decision as to whether such person is being lawfully held prisoner.
HABENDUM - In conveyancing; it is the clause in a deed conveying land which defines the extent of ownership to be held by the grantee.
HEARING - A proceeding whereby the arguments of the interested parties are heared.
HEARSAY - A type of testimony given by a witness who relates, not what he knows personally, but what others have told hi, or what he has heard said by others.
HEARSAY RULE, THE - (a) "Hearsay evidence" is evidence of a statement that was made other than by a witness while testifying at the hearing and that is offered to prove the truth of the matter stated; (b) Except as provided by law, hearsay evidence is inadmissible; (c) This section shall be known and may be cited as the hearsay rule.
HEIR - Generally, one who inherits property, real or personal.
HOLDER OF THE PRIVILEGE - (a) The client when he has no guardian or conservator; (b) A guardian or conservator of the client when the client has a guardian or conservator; (c) The personal representative of the client if the client is dead; (d) A successor, assign, trustee in dissolution, or any similar representative of a firm, association, organization, partnership, business trust, corporation, or public entity that is no longer in existence.
HUNG JURY - One so divided that they can't agree on a verdict.
HUSBAND-WIFE PRIVILEGE - An accused in a criminal proceeding has a privilege to prevent his spouse from testifying against him.
HYPOTHECATE - To pledge a thing without delivering it to the pledgee.
HYPOTHESIS - A supposition, assumption, or toehry.

I

I.E. (id est) - That is.
IB., OR IBID.(ibidem) - In the same place; used to refer to a legal reference previously cited to avoid repeating the entire citation.
ILLICIT - Prohibited; unlawful.
ILLUSORY - Deceiving by false appearance.
IMMUNITY - Exemption.
IMPEACH - To accuse, to dispute.
IMPEDIMENTS - Disabilities, or hindrances.
IMPLEAD - To sue or prosecute by due course of law.
IMPUTED - Attributed or charged to.
IN LOCO PARENTIS - In place of parent, a guardian.
IN TOTO - In the whole; completely.
INCHOATE - Imperfect; unfinished.
INCOMMUNICADO - Denial of the right of a prisoner to communicate with friends or relatives.
INCOMPETENT - One who is incapable of caring for his own affairs because he is mentally deficient or undeveloped.
INCRIMINATION - A matter will incriminate a person if it constitutes, or forms an essential part of, or, taken in connection with other matters disclosed, is a basis for a reasonable inference of such a violation of the laws of this State as to subject him to liability to punishment therefor, unless he has become for any reason permanently immune from punishment for such violation.
INCUMBRANCE - Generally a claim, lien, charge or liability attached to and binding real property.

INDEMNIFY - To secure against loss or damage; also, to make reimbursement to one for a loss already incurred by him.
INDEMNITY - An agreement to reimburse another person in case of an anticipated loss falling upon him.
INDICIA - Signs; indications.
INDICTMENT - An accusation in writing found and presented by a grand jury charging that a person has committed a crime.
INDORSE - To write a name on the back of a legal paper or document, generally, a negotiable instrument
INDUCEMENT - Cause or reason why a thing is done or that which incites the person to do the act or commit a crime; the motive for the criminal act.
INFANT - In civil cases one under 21 years of age.
INFORMATION - A formal accusation of crime made by a prosecuting attorney.
INFRA - Below, under; this word occurring by itself in a publication refers the reader to a future part of the publication.
INGRESS - The act of going into.
INJUNCTION - A writ or order by the court requiring a person, generally, to do or to refrain from doing an act.
INSOLVENT - The condition of a person who is unable to pay his debts.
INSTRUCTION - A direction given by the judge to the jury concerning the law of the case.
INTERIM - In the meantime; time intervening.
INTERLOCUTORY - Temporary, not final; something intervening between the commencement and the end of a suit which decides some point or matter, but is not a final decision of the whole controversy.
INTERROGATORIES - A series of formal written questions used in the examination of a party or a witness usually prior to a trial.
INTESTATE - A person who dies without a will.
INURE - To result, to take effect.
IPSO FACTO - By the fact iself; by the mere fact.
ISSUE (n.) The disputed point or question in a case,

J

JEOPARDY - Danger, hazard, peril.
JOINDER - Joining; uniting with another person in some legal steps or proceeding.
JOINT - United; combined.
JUDGE - Member or members or representative or representatives of a court conducting a trial or hearing at which evidence is introduced.
JUDGMENT - The official decision of a court of justice.
JUDICIAL OR JUDICIARY - Relating to or connected with the administration of justice.
JURAT - The clause written at the foot of an affidavit, stating when, where and before whom such affidavit was sworn.
JURISDICTION - The authority to hear and determine controversies between parties.
JURISPRUDENCE - The philosophy of law.
JURY - A body of persons legally selected to inquire into any matter of fact, and to render their verdict according to the evidence.

L

LACHES - The failure to diligently assert a right, which results in a refusal to allow relief.

LANDLORD AND TENANT - A phrase used to denote the legal relation existing between the owner and occupant of real estate.
LARCENY - Stealing personal property belonging to another.
LATENT - Hidden; that which does not appear on the face of a thing.
LAW - Includes constitutional, statutory, and decisional law.
LAWYER-CLIENT PRIVILEGE - (1) A "client" is a person, public officer, or corporation, association, or other organization or entity, either public or private, who is rendered professional legal services by a lawyer, or who consults a lawyer with a view to obtaining professional legal services from him; (2) A "lawyer" is a person authorized, or reasonably believed by the client to be authorized, to practice law in any state or nation; (3) A "representative of the lawyer" is one employed to assist the lawyer in the rendition of professional legal services; (4) A communication is "confidential" if not intended to be disclosed to third persons other than those to whom disclosure is in furtherance of the rendition of professional legal services to the client or those reasonably necessary for the transmission of the communication.

General rule of privilege - A client has a privilege to refuse to disclose and to prevent any other person from disclosing confidential communications made for the purpose of facilitating the rendition of professional legal services to the client, (1) between himself or his representative and his lawyer or his lawyer's representative, or (2) between his lawyer and the lawyer's representative, or (3) by him or his lawyer to a lawyer representing another in a matter of common interest, or (4) between representatives of the client or between the client and a representative of the client, or (5) between lawyers representing the client.
LEADING QUESTION - Question that suggests to the witness the answer that the examining party desires.
LEASE - A contract by which one conveys real estate for a limited time usually for a specified rent; personal property also may be leased.
LEGISLATION - The act of enacting laws.
LEGITIMATE - Lawful.
LESSEE - One to whom a lease is given.
LESSOR - One who grants a lease
LEVY - A collecting or exacting by authority.
LIABLE - Responsible; bound or obligated in law or equity.
LIBEL (v.) - To defame or injure a person's reputation by a published writing.
 (n.) - The initial pleading on the part of the plaintiff in an admiralty proceeding.
LIEN - A hold or claim which one person has upon the property of another as a security for some debt or charge.
LIQUIDATED - Fixed; settled.
LIS PENDENS - A pending civil or criminal action.
LITERAL - According to the language.
LITIGANT - A party to a lawsuit.
LITATION - A judicial controversy.
LOCUS - A place.
LOCUS DELICTI - Place of the crime.
LOCUS POENITENTIAE - The abandoning or giving up of one's intention to commit some crime before it is fully completed or abandoning a conspiracy before its purpose is accomplished.

M

MALFEASANCE - To do a wrongful act.
MALICE - The doing of a wrongful act Intentionally without just cause or excuse.

MANDAMUS - The name of a writ issued by a court to enforce the performance of some public duty.
MANDATORY (adj.) Containing a command.
MARITIME - Pertaining to the sea or to commerce thereon.
MARSHALING - Arranging or disposing of in order.
MAXIM - An established principle or proposition.
MINISTERIAL - That which involves obedience to instruction, but demands no special discretion, judgment or skill.
MISAPPROPRIATE - Dealing fraudulently with property entrusted to one.
MISDEMEANOR - A crime less than a felony and punishable by a fine or imprisonment for less than one year.
MISFEASANCE - Improper performance of a lawful act.
MISREPRESENTATION - An untrue representation of facts.
MITIGATE - To make or become less severe, harsh.
MITTIMUS - A warrant of commitment to prison.
MOOT (adj.) Unsettled, undecided, not necessary to be decided.
MORTGAGE - A conveyance of property upon condition, as security for the payment of a debt or the performance of a duty, and to become void upon payment or performance according to the stipulated terms.
MORTGAGEE - A person to whom property is mortgaged.
MORTGAGOR - One who gives a mortgage.
MOTION - In legal proceedings, a "motion" is an application, either written or oral, addressed to the court by a party to an action or a suit requesting the ruling of the court on a matter of law.
MUTUALITY - Reciprocation.

N

NEGLIGENCE - The failure to exercise that degree of care which an ordinarily prudent person would exercise under like circumstances.
NEGOTIABLE (instrument) - Any instrument obligating the payment of money which is transferable from one person to another by endorsement and delivery or by delivery only.
NEGOTIATE - To transact business; to transfer a negotiable instrument; to seek agreement for the amicable disposition of a controversy or case.
NOLLE PROSEQUI - A formal entry upon the record, by the plaintiff in a civil suit or the prosecuting officer in a criminal action, by which he declares that he "will no further prosecute" the case.
NOLO CONTENDERE - The name of a plea in a criminal action, having the same effect as a plea of guilty; but not constituting a direct admission of guilt.
NOMINAL - Not real or substantial.
NOMINAL DAMAGES - Award of a trifling sum where no substantial injury is proved to have been sustained.
NONFEASANCE - Neglect of duty.
NOVATION - The substitution of a new debt or obligation for an existing one.
NUNC PRO TUNC - A phrase applied to acts allowed to be done after the time when they should be done, with a retroactive effect.("Now for then.")

O

OATH - Oath includes affirmation or declaration under penalty of perjury.
OBITER DICTUM - Opinion expressed by a court on a matter not essentially involved in a case and hence not a decision; also called dicta, if plural.

OBJECT (v.) - To oppose as improper or illegal and referring the question of its propriety or legality to the court.
OBLIGATION - A legal duty, by which a person is bound to do or not to do a certain thing.
OBLIGEE - The person to whom an obligation is owed.
OBLIGOR - The person who is to perform the obligation.
OFFER (v.) - To present for acceptance or rejection.
    (n.) - A proposal to do a thing, usually a proposal to make a contract.
OFFICIAL INFORMATION - Information within the custody or control of a department or agency of the government the disclosure of which is shown to be contrary to the public interest.
OFFSET - A deduction.
ONUS PROBANDI - Burden of proof.
OPINION - The statement by a judge of the decision reached in a case, giving the law as applied to the case and giving reasons for the judgment; also a belief or view.
OPTION - The exercise of the power of choice; also a privilege existing in one person, for which he has paid money, which gives him the right to buy or sell real or personal property at a given price within a specified time.
ORDER - A rule or regulation; every direction of a court or judge made or entered in writing but not including a judgment.
ORDINANCE - Generally, a rule established by authority; also commonly used to designate the legislative acts of a municipal corporation.
ORIGINAL - Writing or recording itself or any counterpart intended to have the same effect by a person executing or issuing it. An "original" of a photograph includes the negative or any print therefrom. If data are stored in a computer or similar device, any printout or other output readable by sight, shown to reflect the data accurately, is an "original."
OVERT - Open, manifest.

P

PANEL - A group of jurors selected to serve during a term of the court.
PARENS PATRIAE - Sovereign power of a state to protect or be a guardian over children and incompetents.
PAROL - Oral or verbal.
PAROLE - To release one in prison before the expiration of his sentence, conditionally.
PARITY - Equality in purchasing power between the farmer and other segments of the economy.
PARTITION - A legal division of real or personal property between one or more owners.
PARTNERSHIP - An association of two or more persons to carry on as co-owners a business for profit.
PATENT (adj.) - Evident.
    (n.) - A grant of some privilege, property, or authority, made by the government or sovereign of a country to one or more individuals.
PECULATION - Stealing.
PECUNIARY - Monetary.
PENULTIMATE - Next to the last.
PER CURIAM - A phrase used in the report of a decision to distinguish an opinion of the whole court from an opinion written by any one judge.
PER SE - In itself; taken alone.
PERCEIVE - To acquire knowledge through one's senses.
PEREMPTORY - Imperative; absolute.
PERJURY - To lie or state falsely under oath.

PERPETUITY - Perpetual existence; also the quality or condition of an estate limited so that it will not take effect or vest within the period fixed by law.
PERSON - Includes a natural person, firm, association, organization, partnership, business trust, corporation, or public entity.
PERSONAL PROPERTY - Includes money, goods, chattels, things in action, and evidences of debt.
PERSONALTY - Short term for personal property.
PETITION - An application in writing for an order of the court, stating the circumstances upon which it is founded and requesting any order or other relief from a court.
PLAINTIFF - A person who brings a court action.
PLEA - A pleading in a suit or action.
PLEADINGS - Formal allegations made by the parties of their respective claims and defenses, for the judgment of the court.
PLEDGE - A deposit of personal property as a security for the performance of an act.
PLEDGEE - The party to whom goods are delivered in pledge.
PLEDGOR - The party delivering goods in pledge.
PLENARY - Full; complete.
POLICE POWER - Inherent power of the state or its political subdivisions to enact laws within constitutional limits to promote the general welfare of society or the community.
POLLING THE JURY - Call the names of persons on a jury and requiring each juror to declare what his verdict is before it is legally recorded.
POST MORTEM - After death.
POWER OF ATTORNEY - A writing authorizing one to act for another.
PRECEPT - An order, warrant, or writ issued to an officer or body of officers, commanding him or them to do some act within the scope of his or their powers.
PRELIMINARY FACT - Fact upon the existence or nonexistence of which depends the admissibility or inadmissibility of evidence. The phrase "the admissibility or inadmissibility of evidence" includes the qualification or disqualification of a person to be a witness and the existence or nonexistence of a privilege.
PREPONDERANCE - Outweighing.
PRESENTMENT - A report by a grand jury on something they have investigated on their own knowledge.
PRESUMPTION - An assumption of fact resulting from a rule of law which requires such fact to be assumed from another fact or group of facts found or otherwise established in the action.
PRIMA FACUE - At first sight.
PRIMA FACIE CASE - A case where the evidence is very patent against the defendant.
PRINCIPAL - The source of authority or rights; a person primarily liable as differentiated from "principle" as a primary or basic doctrine.
PRO AND CON - For and against.
PRO RATA - Proportionally.
PROBATE - Relating to proof, especially to the proof of wills.
PROBATIVE - Tending to prove.
PROCEDURE - In law, this term generally denotes rules which are established by the Federal, State, or local Governments regarding the types of pleading and courtroom practice which must be followed by the parties involved in a criminal or civil case.
PROCLAMATION - A public notice by an official of some order, intended action, or state of facts.

PROFFERED EVIDENCE - The admissibility or inadmissibility of which is dependent upon the existence or nonexistence of a preliminary fact.
PROMISSORY (NOTE) - A promise in writing to pay a specified sum at an expressed time, or on demand, or at sight, to a named person, or to his order, or bearer.
PROOF - The establishment by evidence of a requisite degree of belief concerning a fact in the mind of the trier of fact or the court.
PROPERTY - Includes both real and personal property.
PROPRIETARY (adj.) - Relating or pertaining to ownership; usually a single owner.
PROSECUTE - To carry on an action or other judicial proceeding; to proceed against a person criminally.
PROVISO - A limitation or condition in a legal instrument.
PROXIMATE - Immediate; nearest
PUBLIC EMPLOYEE - An officer, agent, or employee of a public entity.
PUBLIC ENTITY - Includes a national, state, county, city and county, city, district, public authority, public agency, or any other political subdivision or public corporation, whether foreign or domestic.
PUBLIC OFFICIAL - Includes an official of a political dubdivision of such state or territory and of a municipality.
PUNITIVE - Relating to punishment.

Q

QUASH - To make void.
QUASI - As if; as it were.
QUID PRO QUO - Something for something; the giving of one valuable thing for another.
QUITCLAIM (v.) - To release or relinquish claim or title to, especially in deeds to realty.
QUO WARRANTO - A legal procedure to test an official's right to a public office or the right to hold a franchise, or to hold an office in a domestic corporation.

R

RATIFY - To approve and sanction.
REAL PROPERTY - Includes lands, tenements, and hereditaments.
REALTY - A brief term for real property.
REBUT - To contradict; to refute, especially by evidence and arguments.
RECEIVER - A person who is appointed by the court to receive, and hold in trust property in litigation.
RECIDIVIST - Habitual criminal.
RECIPROCAL - Mutual.
RECOUPMENT - To keep back or get something which is due; also, it is the right of a defendant to have a deduction from the amount of the plaintiff's damages because the plaintiff has not fulfilled his part of the same contract.
RECROSS EXAMINATION - Examination of a witness by a cross-examiner subsequent to a redirect examination of the witness.
REDEEM - To release an estate or article from mortgage or pledge by paying the debt for which it stood as security.
REDIRECT EXAMINATION - Examination of a witness by the direct examiner subsequent to the cross-examination of the witness.
REFEREE - A person to whom a cause pending in a court is referred by the court, to take testimony, hear the parties, and report thereon to the court.

REFERENDUM - A method of submitting an important legislative or administrative matter to a direct vote of the people.
RELEVANT EVIDENCE - Evidence including evidence relevant to the credulity of a witness or hearsay declarant, having any tendency in reason to prove or disprove any disputed fact that is of consequence to the determination of the action.
REMAND - To send a case back to the lower court from which it came, for further proceedings.
REPLEVIN - An action to recover goods or chattels wrongfully taken or detained.
REPLY (REPLICATION) - Generally, a reply is what the plaintiff or other person who has instituted proceedings says in answer to the defendant's case.
RE JUDICATA - A thing judicially acted upon or decided.
RES ADJUDICATA - Doctrine that an issue or dispute litigated and determined in a case between the opposing parties is deemed permanently decided between these parties.
RESCIND (RECISSION) - To avoid or cancel a contract.
RESPONDENT - A defendant in a proceeding in chancery or admiralty; also, the person who contends against the appeal in a case.
RESTITUTION - In equity, it is the restoration of both parties to their original condition (when practicable), upon the rescission of a contract for fraud or similar cause.
RETROACTIVE (RETROSPECTIVE) - Looking back; effective as of a prior time.
REVERSED - A term used by appellate courts to indicate that the decision of the lower court in the case before it has been set aside.
REVOKE - To recall or cancel.
RIPARIAN (RIGHTS) - The rights of a person owning land containing or bordering on a water course or other body of water, such as lakes and rivers.

S

SALE - A contract whereby the ownership of property is transferred from one person to another for a sum of money or for any consideration.
SANCTION - A penalty or punishment provided as a means of enforcing obedience to a law; also, an authorization.
SATISFACTION - The discharge of an obligation by paying a party what is due to him; or what is awarded to him by the judgment of a court or otherwise.
SCIENTER - Knowingly; also, it is used in pleading to denote the defendant's guilty knowledge.
SCINTILLA - A spark; also the least particle.
SECRET OF STATE - Governmental secret relating to the national defense or the international relations of the United States.
SECURITY - Indemnification; the term is applied to an obligation, such as a mortgage or deed of trust, given by a debtor to insure the payment or performance of his debt, by furnishing the creditor with a resource to be used in case of the debtor's failure to fulfill the principal obligation.
SENTENCE - The judgment formally pronounced by the court or judge upon the defendant after his conviction in a criminal prosecution.
SET-OFF - A claim or demand which one party in an action credits against the claim of the opposing party.
SHALL and MAY - "Shall" is mandatory and "may" is permissive.
SITUS - Location.
SOVEREIGN - A person, body or state in which independent and supreme authority is vested.
STARE DECISIS - To follow decided cases.

STATE - "State" means this State, unless applied to the different parts of the United States. In the latter case, it includes any state, district, commonwealth, territory or insular possession of the United States, including the District of Columbia.

STATEMENT - (a) Oral or written verbal expression or (b) nonverbal conduct of a person intended by him as a substitute for oral or written verbal expression.

STATUTE - An act of the legislature. Includes a treaty.

STATUTE OF LIMITATION - A statute limiting the time to bring an action after the right of action has arisen.

STAY - To hold in abeyance an order of a court.

STIPULATION - Any agreement made by opposing attorneys regulating any matter incidental to the proceedings or trial.

SUBORDINATION (AGREEMENT) - An agreement making one's rights inferior to or of a lower rank than another's.

SUBORNATION - The crime of procuring a person to lie or to make false statements to a court.

SUBPOENA - A writ or order directed to a person, and requiring his attendance at a particular time and place to testify as a witness.

SUBPOENA DUCES TECUM - A subpoena used, not only for the purpose of compelling witnesses to attend in court, but also requiring them to bring with them books or documents which may be in their possession, and which may tend to elucidate the subject matter of the trial.

SUBROGATION - The substituting of one for another as a creditor, the new creditor succeeding to the former's rights.

SUBSIDY - A government grant to assist a private enterprise deemed advantageous to the public.

SUI GENERIS - Of the same kind.

SUIT - Any civil proceeding by a person or persons against another or others in a court of justice by which the plaintiff pursues the remedies afforded him by law.

SUMMONS - A notice to a defendant that an action against him has been commenced and requiring him to appear in court and answer the complaint.

SUPRA - Above; this word occurring by itself in a book refers the reader to a previous part of the book.

SURETY - A person who binds himself for the payment of a sum of money, or for the performance of something else, for another.

SURPLUSAGE - Extraneous or unnecessary matter.

SURVIVORSHIP - A term used when a person becomes entitled to property by reason of his having survived another person who had an interest in the property.

SUSPEND SENTENCE - Hold back a sentence pending good behavior of prisoner.

SYLLABUS - A note prefixed to a report, especially a case, giving a brief statement of the court's ruling on different issues of the case.

T

TALESMAN - Person summoned to fill a panel of jurors.

TENANT - One who holds or possesses lands by any kind of right or title; also, one who has the temporary use and occupation of real property owned by another person (landlord), the duration and terms of his tenancy being usually fixed by an instrument called "a lease."

TENDER - An offer of money; an expression of willingness to perform a contract according to its terms.

TERM - When used with reference to a court, it signifies the period of time during which the court holds a session, usually of several weeks or months duration.

TESTAMENTARY - Pertaining to a will or the administration of a will.
TESTATOR (male)
TESTATRIX (female) - One who makes or has made a testament or will.
TESTIFY (TESTIMONY) - To give evidence under oath as a witness.
TO WIT - That is to say; namely.
TORT - Wrong; injury to the person.
TRANSITORY - Passing from place to place.
TRESPASS - Entry into another's ground, illegally.
TRIAL - The examination of a cause, civil or criminal, before a judge who has jurisdiction over it, according to the laws of the land.
TRIER OF FACT - Includes (a) the jury and (b) the court when the court is trying an issue of fact other than one relating to the admissibility of evidence.
TRUST - A right of property, real or personal, held by one party for the benefit of another.
TRUSTEE - One who lawfully holds property in custody for the benefit of another.

U

UNAVAILABLE AS A WITNESS - The declarant is (1) Exempted or precluded on the ground of privilege from testifying concerning the matter to which his statement is relevant; (2) Disqualified from testifying to the matter; (3) Dead or unable to attend or to testify at the hearing because of then existing physical or mental illness or infirmity; (4) Absent from the hearing and the court is unable to compel his attendance by its process; or (5) Absent from the hearing and the proponent of his statement has exercised reasonable diligence but has been unable to procure his attendance by the court's process.
ULTRA VIRES - Acts beyond the scope and power of a corporation, association, etc.
UNILATERAL - One-sided; obligation upon, or act of one party.
USURY - Unlawful interest on a loan.

V

VACATE - To set aside; to move out.
VARIANCE - A discrepancy or disagreement between two instruments or two aspects of the same case, which by law should be consistent.
VENDEE - A purchaser or buyer.
VENDOR - The person who transfers property by sale, particularly real estate; the term "seller" is used more commonly for one who sells personal property.
VENIREMEN - Persons ordered to appear to serve on a jury or composing a panel of jurors.
VENUE - The place at which an action is tried, generally based on locality or judicial district in which an injury occurred or a material fact happened.
VERDICT - The formal decision or finding of a jury.
VERIFY - To confirm or substantiate by oath.
VEST - To accrue to.
VOID - Having no legal force or binding effect.
VOIR DIRE - Preliminary examination of a witness or a juror to test competence, interest, prejudice, etc.

W

WAIVE - To give up a right.
WAIVER - The intentional or voluntary relinquishment of a known right.
WARRANT (WARRANTY) (v.) - To promise that a certain fact or state of facts, in relation to the subject matter, is, or shall be, as it is represented to be.

WARRANT (n.) - A writ issued by a judge, or other competent authority, addressed to a sheriff, or other officer, requiring him to arrest the person therein named, and bring him before the judge or court to answer or be examined regarding the offense with which he is charged.

WRIT - An order or process issued in the name of the sovereign or in the name of a court or judicial officer, commanding the performance or nonperformance of some act.

WRITING - Handwriting, typewriting, printing, photostating, photographing and every other means of recording upon any tangible thing any form of communication or representation, including letters, words, pictures, sounds, or symbols, or combinations thereof.

WRITINGS AND RECORDINGS - Consists of letters, words, or numbers, or their equivalent, set down by handwriting, typewriting, printing, photostating, photographing, magnetic impulse, mechanical or electronic recording, or other form of data compilation.

Y

YEA AND NAY - Yes and no.

YELLOW DOG CONTRACT - A contract by which employer requires employee to sign an instrument promising as condition that he will not join a union during its continuance, and will be discharged if he does join.

Z

ZONING - The division of a city by legislative regulation into districts and the prescription and application in each district of regulations having to do with structural and architectural designs of buildings and of regulations prescribing use to which buildings within designated districts may be put.

www.ingramcontent.com/pod-product-compliance
Lightning Source LLC
Chambersburg PA
CBHW080734230426
43665CB00020B/2738